N O W
FOR THE
DISAPPOINTING
PART

NOW FOR THE DISAPPOINTING PART

A Pseudo-Adult's Decade of Short-Term Jobs, Long-Term Relationships, and Holding Out for Something Better

STEVEN BARKER

Skyhorse Publishing

A version of "Temporary Madness" appeared in *Salon*, March 8, 2015, as "Jeff Bezos relies on lowly grunts like me: Life as a cog in the Amazon machine." A version of "Now for the Disappointing Part" appeared in *The Weeklings*, March 21, 2014, as "What Can Brown Do For Me?" A version of "American Temp" appeared in *Split Lip* magazine, issue 17, January–March, 2014.

Skyhorse Publishing books may be purchased in bulk at special discounts for sales promotion, corporate gifts, fund-raising, or educational purposes. Special editions can also be created to specifications. For details, contact the Special Sales Department, Skyhorse Publishing, 307 West 36th Street, 11th Floor, New York, NY 10018 or info@skyhorsepublishing.com.

Skyhorse® and Skyhorse Publishing® are registered trademarks of Skyhorse Publishing, Inc.®, a Delaware corporation.

Visit our website at www.skyhorsepublishing.com.

10 9 8 7 6 5 4 3 2 1

Library of Congress Cataloging-in-Publication Data is available on file.

Cover design by Brian Peterson

Print ISBN: 978-1-5107-1082-5
Ebook ISBN: 978-1-5107-1084-9

Printed in the United States of America

Can't be king of the world,
if you're a slave to the grind.

—Skid Row

Contents

Preface

By some definitions I am a millennial. I was born in 1980 and entered adulthood in the early 2000s, and my transition from child to adult lasted over a decade. However, I don't identify as a millennial. If I had been born five months earlier I would have been branded Generation X, a label I don't feel a strong connection to either. And no brand-savvy sociologist came up with a term catchy enough to enter the zeitgeist for the in-betweeners born on the cusp.

I listened to Beck's *Mellow Gold* album and watched *Beavis and Butt-head* in eighth grade, I had a beeper in high school, and during my senior year of college I was on Friendster and made Fruity Loop beats on my laptop. Granted, I did spend five and half years in college, which I excuse due to the fact that I transferred schools in the middle of my junior year and lost a bunch of credits, but that only accounts for one additional year. The extra half was due to the fact that I got a 1.9, second semester freshman year. I partied too much and regularly skipped all but one of my classes. I would have flunked out had I not pulled an A in English 102. Side note: *My mother would like me to point out I did not repeat that mistake and ended a number of semesters on the academic Dean's List.*

Experiencing a few bonus semesters allowed me to fall back with the millennial front-runners, while the tail end of Gen X'ers moved ahead of me. I got a taste of both generations. I drank Zima in the nineties and Sparks in 2000, and was underage on both occasions. Yet neither experience defined me more than the other. I didn't know where I fit in, a feeling that has continued throughout my life.

My parents were baby boomers and they flawlessly executed the movement from kids to adults to parents. They were early into their college careers when they met at a party where my dad was playing drums for a Stones cover band called The Shooters. They married a few years later after receiving their bachelor's degrees and landing jobs at IBM. My dad worked his way up to a point where they could buy a house and my mom could quit working to have my brother. Four years later there was me, and then four years after that my sister.

I just turned thirty-six. When my dad was my age he was a husband, a father of three, a homeowner, and the manager of administration and distribution for IBM's Southeast Asia region. Last night, I ate peanut butter and jelly on a hot dog bun for dinner.

My father's structured path of college, marriage, home ownership, and kids is still followed by a few. But whether it's Generation X or millennials, it's no longer the norm. The opportunity to land a starting-level position in a company that nurtures its workers as they move up the corporate ladder is less prevalent, because companies no longer invest in their employees, instead opting to cut costs and increase profit by hiring disposable temps. Home ownership is difficult for anyone less than upper-middle class. And the debt attached to every college grad can make starting a family financially impossible.

All of that can be applied to me, but it's not necessarily the reason for my extended transition from child to adult. Career, home ownership, and family were not my goals. After college, my friends made decisions that would affect the rest of their lives, while I couldn't find anything worthy of a long-term commitment. I had an English degree with an emphasis in creative writing. I knew I wanted to write, but at twenty-three years old I hadn't had the chance to explore *what* it was I wanted to write. Temping and the time between contracts gave me that opportunity.

As a result my life was unstable, but no matter how bad it got I could always find comfort in knowing that I hadn't committed to the wrong thing. I was able to manage my uncertain circumstances, but it was difficult for someone else to share the life. People who loved me eventually grew tired of my inability to plan for the future and left.

Being that I'm single, rent a one-bedroom apartment, and don't have kids or a career path, I fit the mold of a millennial. It's just that my situation has been based on choice and not so much the result of a system that no longer offers a clear path to the American Dream. So, sure I'm a millennial, even if I've never Snapchatted a taco. Although it could be argued my circumstances are a result of the apathy associated with Generation X. The most accurate way to describe it would be to say I'm both and I'm neither. Just as I'm Canadian, yet I have lived in America the majority of my life. My American friends all call me Canadian and my Canadian friends call me American. I'm both and I'm neither. As a temp working alongside full-time employees, I was their coworker, but not really. That lack of identity made it impossible for me to know what I wanted, because I didn't know who I was.

This book is a look over my shoulder at the ten-year period following my graduation from college where I committed to nothing, believing it was better to abandon an okay situation, because the next one could potentially be better. Though I didn't know that's what I was doing at the time. Clarity is hard to achieve inside a vacuum. You will read about my experiences working a variety of temporary jobs, intertwined with details about my unsuccessful romantic relationships, written with the luxury of hindsight.

Names have been changed and dialogue has been written to my best recollection. Certain details that I didn't believe were mine to share have been left out. Although nothing was omitted for the purpose of making myself look good. I have made mistakes and I have hurt people I love. There are times you might disagree with my actions, but it's my hope you will appreciate my honesty.

PART I

5:00 a.m.

The alarm clock chops through your slumber and you peel your eyes open. It's 5:00 a.m. You hit snooze, then lie there with the blanket pulled up to your chin as you stare at the ceiling until the alarm sounds again. You dread the chill that comes with removing the covers at dawn.

The gentle drip of the kitchen coffeemaker signals the day has begun. You set it last night to shave a minute off the morning routine. It was a gift from your ex-girlfriend. She knew before you did that you needed a coffeemaker with a timer on it. She was thoughtful like that. Even though you know the breakup was probably for the best, the bed feels too big on mornings like this.

The need to piss becomes unbearable, and you get up. The bathroom is dark, but you've done this so many times you know exactly where to aim. The fierce bubbling sound lets you know that you're on target.

You assemble a turkey sandwich, seal it in a Tupperware, and delicately place the knife in the sink. You do all of this on light feet because every noise is amplified at this hour, and you don't want to disturb your neighbors. You're not sure why, though, since you weren't provided the same courtesy five hours earlier. The guy in the apartment below is learning guitar. You've noticed his progress. Last night he made it all the way through "Smoke on the Water" without a mistake. You wonder why you've never dedicated yourself to something.

The showerhead sprays cold buckshot into your chest even though you deemed it hot enough when you hung your toes under the faucet. You twist the knob until it's too hot—burning almost—then bring it down just a notch below scalding.

You towel off while keeping an eye on the clock. You're on schedule to make the early bus. You scan your closet trying to remember which of your four work shirts you wore the previous day and remember it was the black one with thin gray stripes. You know this because your boss was wearing something similar, and you were embarrassed when a coworker commented on the fact. You choose the navy-blue one—it's not your favorite because it hangs a little too low and you have never been able to determine if it should be tucked in or not. If you decide to go out after work, you'll change, but you're almost certain that after work you'll go for a run, then watch *Seinfeld* reruns until bed.

You double-check the door, since you don't live in a secure building. It doesn't budge when you give it a hefty push, and you are satisfied it's locked. You hit play on the latest episode of *This American Life*. You listen to an ad for Squarespace because you don't want to take the phone out of your pocket to skip the commercials when walking through the alley. A man trying on a purple hoodie he pulled from the Dumpster looks you up and down as you pass.

Most of the faces are familiar at this hour—there's the guy in scrubs who's always chomping on a PowerBar, and the tall blonde who wears a long coat and walks with her chin up. Over the past week the smile you share in passing has grown wider. You've considered slipping her a note with an invitation to coffee, but know a gesture so brash is out of your comfort zone. Instead, you anticipate the day you'll come across her on Tinder and swipe right. Then there's the woman who smokes on the corner with a Starbucks cup. She takes long drawn-out puffs through a smirk like she's looking forward to the day ahead of her. You take a deep breath when cutting through her cloud of smoke, hoping to inhale some of her optimism.

You know you're on time when you see the girl who always wears flats, even when it's cold, standing at the bus stop. You recognize her because you both like to stand in the back of the bus, even if there's an open seat. You prefer standing since you know you're about to spend the next eight hours sitting at a desk. You also like the back because of the unobstructed window that faces east when the bus crosses the 520 Bridge. It's best in early February because the mountains are backlit by an orange sky. You savor that moment and hold on to it as long as you can while wishing it could somehow last longer. You wonder if it has become so repetitive the other bus riders are bored with it or if they've never actually noticed the beauty.

You're the first to exit when the bus reaches your stop, but you don't take the most direct route to your building because the episode of *This American Life* you're listening to is just getting good. It's a piece about internet trolls. Lindy

West has just confronted her worst one, and you want to hear how it ends.

You swipe your badge. It's a distinct color that advertises your temporary status. You smile and nod at the coworker you know and pretend to look at a sign for a blood drive when you pass that one guy with a corner office. You assume he's important because he's the only person on the floor who regularly wears a tie, and the color of his badge means he doesn't know the date he'll clock out for the final time.

You get to your desk and turn on your computer before taking off your coat. When the green available notification appears next to your screen name, you walk down the hall for coffee. You're thankful no one is in the break room because it's too early for small talk.

You return to your desk and place your coffee mug on top of a ring stain and think that you should find the time to wipe down your workspace.

There are twenty-three messages in your inbox, and your first meeting of the day was moved up one hour. You drag the cursor over the first email, think back to the sunrise, and wonder what it would look like from the top of the mountains. You promise yourself one day you'll find out, then click your mouse.

Like Barker, Like Barton

Six months into my freshman year of college, I was taken with Boston. I loved riding the T across the city and spending brisk New England afternoons smoking cigarettes and looking for records on Newbury Street. It was my choice whether to attend a bio lecture or ditch it to sit on a park bench with a brunette in a peacoat and talk about Emily Dickinson's unconventional capitalization.

My phone rang one Thursday afternoon in the final month of the semester.

"Steven, it's your father." Long before I ever moved out for college I'd become accustomed to speaking with my father long-distance. Calls started one of two ways—"Hi, son," which meant we were going to have a pleasant conversation about hockey or music, or the aforementioned "Steven, it's your father," which meant he had a few drinks and missed me and just wanted to make sure I knew he loved me. I received these calls throughout my childhood. He was usually in a hotel room somewhere in Latin America on a business trip and worried he was being an absent father. This was the first time he was home and I was away.

I rolled my eyes at my roommate and handed him the joint we were in the middle of smoking. *Too bad there's no caller ID in the dorms*, I thought. I walked out of my room, away from the guys playing dice beneath a cloud of smoke, to escape the room-rattling thump of the Wu-Tang Clan's "C.R.E.A.M."

"I have news," my dad said.

My dad felt like he always needed to have a reason to call me, so when he just wanted to catch up he'd open with some news or a question as an excuse to get a conversation started. Two weeks earlier he wanted to know if I could explain the difference between "hip-hop" and "rap." But I could tell by the tone of his voice that this news was more than just a conversation starter.

"We're moving to San Diego."

I learned my ABCs in Hong Kong, had my first kiss in Toronto, and graduated high school in Connecticut. Moving around was so typical with my family that we were often mistaken for military.

"Like, California?" I asked, not sure if my buzz had caused me to misunderstand him.

"I'm moving out there in a week, and your mother will follow with your sister at the end of August. How would you like to spend your summer on the West Coast?"

Everything I knew about California came from watching *90210*. I would sit in my parents' basement with a flannel blanket as sleet pounded the cellar door and I wished I could play volleyball on the beach with Steve Sanders, while a bikini-clad Kelly Taylor cheered us on.

"I could get you a job at the plant where I will be the new vice president," he continued.

I didn't know what it meant to work in a plant, but it sounded a little more involved than what I was looking for in a summer job. The previous summer I'd been a stock boy in a wine shop and could get away with reading *Spin* magazine in the basement on lazy afternoons. Just the word "plant" brought up images of sweaty guys in hard hats shoveling coal into a furnace.

"We could probably get you a car," he said. "So you'll have something to get you to and from work."

"Interesting." I had watched all my friends get brand-new cars for their sixteenth birthday. My high school parking lot looked like a car show, except for the teachers' lot that was filled with ten-year-old Hondas with missing hubcaps. Unlike the majority of my classmates, my license hadn't come with a new car. My Friday nights always began on the phone negotiating a ride to the party. I had access to my mom's SUV for school and picking up my little sister from soccer practice, but I spent most of my teenage years as a passenger. I was accustomed to being carless and believed that the only way I'd ever have my own wheels was if I bought them myself, which didn't seem plausible until long after college.

"Take a day to think about it and let me know."

I returned to my room. There was still a pinch left on the joint. I inhaled until it burned my fingers, then announced to the room, in my best Notorious B.I.G. voice, "I'm going to Cali, strictly for the weather, women, and weed, sticky green, no seeds bitch, please."

•

My father met me at the arrival gate sporting tanned skin and a pair of Ray-Bans tucked into the open neck of a Tommy Bahama shirt. It was hard to imagine he was raised by parents who never graduated high school in a house whose only source of heat during Quebec winters was the oven that cooked their food.

"You're going to need a good pair of sunglasses," he said and then looked at my pasty Canadian legs. "And a *lot* of sunscreen."

In the parking lot he popped the trunk of a silver Audi TT from a key in his pocket.

"Is that your car?" I asked.

"There's only about ten of these in North America right now and only two this color. I had to place my order months ago."

"Quite a step up from the Gremlin you had when I was born."

As we drove through the city, Dad took on the role of tour guide. He'd already been there a month, and I could tell he was eager to show me around. Growing up in East Coast Canada, California always felt like a mythical land.

"That's In-and-Out Burger. You're going to want to try that at some point. You can see the ocean right over there. Any interest in learning to surf?"

"Sure."

It was so exactly as I imagined that it felt clichéd. Women with golden abs ran along the street in sports bras and matching shorts. Kids rode longboards shirtless and shoeless, and all the cars looked like they'd just been driven off the lot. A bright red Volkswagen with blonde hair blowing out of the front and back window zoomed past us.

"I'm not so sure I'll fit in here," I said.

"Lucky for you, work ends at 3:30. You'll have your afternoons free to figure that out."

"Short work day," I said.

"Work starts at 7:00."

"A.m.?"

"Of course."

I was used to oversleeping for noon classes and, on Sundays, sometimes didn't get out of bed until 5:00 p.m. The last time I saw 7:00 a.m. I was drinking Captain Morgan with a townie who thought I was exotic because I had travelled to three different continents before I was six years old.

"You lived in Hong Kong. What was it like?" she asked me as we stood in the corner of a dimly lit basement party.

"Crowded."

Two hours later we were sitting in my bed, and she shared her dream of escaping Boston for Los Angeles. When the sun rose she left for work at the bagel shop down the street; I passed out for the next eleven hours.

My father explained I'd be working on an assembly line for ruggedized computers, under the alias Steven Barton. He didn't want anyone to know I was the VP's son. It seemed exciting to take on a new persona. I thought about making a fake background for Mr. Barton. Maybe he was a computer major looking to be the next Bill Gates, or maybe he was in culinary school with dreams of opening his own restaurant that only served eggs Benedict. Then I figured it would be easiest just to fit in and say I was a general studies major at the local community college.

Saturday morning we woke up early to look at used cars. According to my dad's rules, our budget was ten thousand dollars, and the car must have air bags and get good gas mileage.

I was interested in a Volkswagen Golf, but my dad told me a sedan had better resale value. Even though he had recently made the jump from upper middle class to upper-upper middle class, he was still cautious with money. Growing up in a house that sometimes went winters without heat made him frugal. I figured it would be easy to find a decent car for that price.

Golf or not, I was psyched on Volkswagen. I grew up thinking they were the coolest cars, only because Mike D of the Beastie Boys wore a Volkswagen emblem around his neck in the eighties.

My dad pulled the Audi into a VW dealership, and three guys in pressed shirts and ties swarmed the car. One guy broke from the pack opening the driver's side door.

"Great ride. Those are hard to come by. You must have some connections," he said, admiring the sleek design that shined in the sun. "I'm Tony. How can I serve you guys today?" He had an Australian accent.

"We're just looking," my father said, with a bored look draped across his face.

We casually walked through the lot, and I kept my eyes open for a sticker ten thousand dollars or below, eventually stopping at an $8,999 maroon Jetta.

"How about a test run?" Tony suggested.

I pulled onto the highway, and as I got comfortable with the car, my father grilled Tony.

"Was the previous owner a smoker? Smells kind of funny. How's the wiring? I hear Volkswagens have bad wiring. What's the resale on a maroon car? I can't image there's a lot of people dying for a maroon car."

"Actually it's burgundy," Tony said.

"How's the resale on a burgundy car?"

"Burgundy is a hot color right now," he said and then looked over at me. "How's it feel?"

I'd already been coached not to show interest, but it was moot. I liked how it handled, but I had no interest in a maroon car. It was closer to the type of car found in the teachers' lot of my high school than the students'. I wanted something red, white, or black that would blend in with the other cars zipping up and down the Pacific Coast Highway.

"Not for me," I said and shrugged as I pulled the key from the ignition.

We stopped in at another dealership where my dad small-talked with a salesman just to get his business card.

"It's important to have options, son," he said slipping the salesman's business card into a stack he kept tucked into his shirt pocket.

"Did you like the handling of the Jetta?"

"Yeah, I just didn't like the maroon."

"Maroon cars are for divorced high school algebra teachers."

We drove back to the first dealership.

"Back so soon," Tony said with an eager smile splashed across his face.

"We'd like to check out another used Jetta," my dad said.

We followed Tony to a seventeen-thousand-dollar silver Jetta. "This is one of our best preowned Jettas. An old lady leased it for a year and only drove to the grocery store and back. Still has that new car smell."

"We're looking for something in the nine-thousand-dollar range," my dad said. "His mother is hoping I spend less than that."

I was getting worried we wouldn't find anything when my dad called me over to a black Jetta with a sticker price of thirteen thousand.

"Looks great, but isn't that over the budget?"

"Let just take it for a spin," my dad said.

While my dad and Tony formed a friendship, I drove around aimlessly. Tony explained he was born in Australia and had moved to the States a few years prior. He was a mechanic, but was now more interested in selling cars than working on them. My dad had spent two years living in Australia on business and was able to bond with Tony over their shared love of the Sydney Swans.

"You're the first person I've met in America who's interested in Australian rules football," Tony said.

"I had season tickets. I follow them online now. I can't find a network that airs the matches."

"I know of a great bar that has a satellite. We should go together sometime."

"If they sell meat pies, I'm there."

When we returned to the dealership, my father said we were interested, but not for the sticker price.

"I can only go as low as $12,500," Tony said.

"That's too much. His mother would kill me if I went a penny over $9,750."

"If I beg my boss, I can maybe go as low as $12,250. But only because you're a fellow Swans fan."

My dad reached into his front pocket and pulled out a stack of business cards. "Thanks Tony, but that's just too high." He flipped through the stack of cards and made sure to keep the other salesman's business card prominently displayed on top. He pulled his own card from the bottom of the stack and handed it to Tony. "Here's my card. Call me if you change your mind."

My dad and I turned to leave when Tony stopped us to make his final counter.

"I can do eleven thousand dollars!"

"Sold," my dad said.

A week later my older brother saw the Jetta and said, "Dude, that's a chick car."

On my first day of work I was shown around by Darnell, who had a shaved head except for a chunk in the back, which he braided into a tight ponytail. He gave me a smock and showed me to my station, where I'd be drilling fans into the backs of hard drives. To my left, a squat, round-faced woman named Suni installed the fans, and a short guy, who couldn't seem to help grinning all the time and reminded me of an Ewok, attached covers over them. His name badge read JERRY, but he introduced himself as Yeddy. The day was broken up with two fifteen-minute breaks and thirty minutes for lunch.

The line started, and I drilled four screws, one in each corner of the fan, and then passed it along. The second I pushed the completed chassis to my right, a new one appeared. It didn't seem like much at first, and using a power drill was kind of fun. I got into a rhythm and started talking with Suni.

"You look so young" was the first thing she said to me.

"I'm twenty. I'm on break from college."

"College is good."

"I like it."

"You don't party all the time like some kids, do you?"

"Never."

"My nephew went to college—my brother pays a lot of money. He drinks every night then gets sent home with no refund."

"I've seen kids like that," I said. "What a waste of their parents' money."

We went back to drilling, and after what could've been five minutes or two hours, Suni spoke again.

"Watch out for Yeddy. He's the joker around here."

"Lies," Jerry said, then looked over at me and winked.

"What are you doing for lunch today, Yeddy?" she asked.

"My wife made me balut."

"Steven, do you eat balut?" Suni asked me.

"I'm not sure what that is," I said. I'd never heard the word before, but the way it sounded, *baal-oot*, didn't sound appetizing. It sounded like a part of the animal most people throw away.

"You wouldn't like balut," Jerry said. He scrunched up his face, which enhanced his resemblance to an Ewok. "You wouldn't like balut," he repeated.

"What is it?" Now I was intrigued.

"You will have to just try it." Suni laughed.

I spent most of the time listening to their conversations and not participating because I didn't have much to contribute on the subject of child rearing. They knew the names of each other's kids, the schools they attended, and grades they were in. It was the type of intimate coworker relationship I'd never spent long enough at a job to develop. I imagined they rarely saw each other outside of the warehouse except for the occasional BBQ, where the awkwardness of the real world drove all their small talk to the subject of work. Yet while at work they only talked about their lives outside it.

"They ask me, 'Mommy, how do I finish this problem?' I don't know," Suni said, then laughed. "I don't know why the teacher expects me to teach them how to do algebra. I'm not the teacher."

When they did address me it was usually to tell me to slow down. They had a rhythm they'd perfected over the years and expected me to adapt.

"Less mistakes when we're all on the same pace," Yeddy said.

I looked at the clock.

11:40.

I discovered that I drilled eight screws a minute and did the math in my head, counting how many screws I did in an hour, then in a day, then in a week, then how many I would complete over the two and half months I was Steven Barton. I lost count when I started wondering where all these computers were going. How many of these get produced a day? Will there ever be a time when Jerry doesn't have another chassis to push my way? How did man evolve from apes to end up like this?

I felt my chest tighten. I took deep breaths and tried to calm down by looking out the window to remind myself I was just two hours south of 90210, the place I dreamed about in my cold childhood basement. My eyes followed the gray brick wall, scanning for a window, but there wasn't one. Just cement that seemed to go on forever. I was in a dungeon with different sections where people were hammering and drilling and soldering pieces of metal. I'd actually died in the plane ride to California and was in hell. I was going to spend eternity with a drill in my hand, screwing in fans that would never be turned on, just disassembled and sent right back to me. The sounds of saws and conveyor belts poked at my eardrum, and I thought I was going to have a panic attack when someone yelled, "Lunch!"

I started to rush to my car for my peanut butter and jelly sandwich, but before I made it out the door, Darnell stopped me.

"How's it going so far?" he asked.

"Better than shoveling snow."

"If you do a good job we can think about moving you to a more challenging station. There's a lot for room for growth here."

"Okay," I said, barely listening. I had PB&J on the brain and thought about how good a cigarette was going to taste with the flavor of peanut butter still lingering on my tongue.

"We're going to play some half court if you want to join us."

"I'll sit this one out."

I sat in my car and wolfed down my warm sandwich as I quietly listened to an Eminem cassette.

I thought about driving off and never coming back. If I really were Steven Barton, I probably would have. Steven Barton wouldn't have to explain himself to my father. Steven Barton would be pulling into the beach with a surfboard strapped to the roof of his car and a cooler full of cold ones in the trunk. Steven Barton was *wicked fresh*.

Steven Barker smoked a few cigarettes while sitting on the curb and watching the guys play basketball. They were throwing elbows and boxing out in the paint. At 12:30 everyone headed back in and the victors high-fived.

"Maybe we need to switch up the teams since you guys suck so bad," someone called across the room.

"Maybe you should shut your mouth!" someone else responded.

"Yo momma didn't last night," another guy called out.

"You only won because Ferdinano's hungover."

As the group transitioned back into work mode, the trash talk died down, and the rhythm of the assembly line returned to the same pace we'd left before the break. I was reminded of the nightly soccer games I played in Boston during exam week. My friends and I would gather in the gym for an hour of competitive cardio to release the stress brought on by hours of studying and then kick back with a beer while the winning team told the losers how much they sucked.

I missed those games and wondered what my outlet for the summer would be. My only social contacts were Suni and Jerry. They were pleasant enough, but I doubted that either one would want to spend an evening kicking around a ball and then splitting a case of beer.

That night my dad and I went to a bar and grill that overlooked the ocean. Our waitress had a yoga-toned body tucked into a pair of black short shorts and a tiny top. She asked me what I was studying in school, and I blushed when I said I wanted to be a writer. "Good luck," she said then recommended the avocado burger. She laughed when I told her I'd never had avocado before. "In California we put avocado on everything," she said.

"How was work?" my dad asked.

"Awful."

"What was so bad about it?"

"It's boring. I do the same thing over and over."

"Is it hard?"

"Not really."

"Do they treat you well?"

"Everyone seems nice."

"I don't see the problem."

"It just sucks," I said.

The waitress returned with a Coke for me and a beer for my dad.

"Order another beer and let me have that one," I said.

"That would be dishonest. You can have a beer back at the condo."

"After the day I had I deserve a beer."

"I'm sure it wasn't so bad."

"I did the same thing over and over. Time went by so slow. It was slower than church time."

"You know, son." *Here we go*, I thought. Whenever my father called me "son" some sort of life lesson always followed, or a reminder of how easy my life was compared to his when he was my age. I already knew about the two-hour bus ride he took to high school and how he was the first in his family to graduate college and how he started out in the IBM mailroom and worked his way up to being a top salesman and blah, fuckity, blah.

"When I was your age," he began, "I got a job at a meat packing plant for $2.50 an hour. In 1967, that was good money.

"I had a few different jobs there, but the one I hated most was removing the pig intestines, then wrapping them around a pole. I had to wear rubber boots because I stood in blood and waste two inches thick. The smell was awful, and my fingers were numb from the cold. I was the youngest person working there and the only one who was in college. The guys I worked with had been there for years and would continue to be there for the rest of their lives. And they were happy with that because it meant they could pay rent, feed their kids, and have a little left over to spend at the bar. Most of them never made it past the eighth grade.

"They resented me and called me 'college boy.' They hazed me by stuffing discarded pig ends into my peanut butter and jelly sandwich. Most days I went without lunch because I couldn't afford to eat in the cafeteria."

"Gross," I said.

"When work ended on Friday night and I got on the bus to go back to my parents' house, I already dreaded Monday morning. But you know what?" He stopped himself and took a long sip of his beer. "I was grateful for the work. I made enough money that summer to move into my fraternity house and take your mother out to dinner. It's possible that you might not have been born without that job."

"I'd puke if I had to touch a pig intestine," I said.

"I'm not telling you this to make you feel bad or say I had it harder. I just want you to know about me at your age. I'm happy you don't have to handle dead pigs all day. I didn't eat pork for fifteen years after that job. Most jobs aren't fun, but lucky for you, you're in college and hopefully will have much better job opportunities when you graduate. And if you really hate this job that much and you find something better, by all means, you should take it. But you will work this summer. Plus, don't you want to go back to Boston in the fall with some extra money so you can do fun things with your friends?"

"Yeah."

The waitress brought us our meals, and I was in love with my avocado burger on the first bite. *How have I never had this before?* I thought.

We ate and watched surfers squeeze in a few after-work waves. As the sun set, my dad turned his head toward the horizon. "I can get used to this."

A few weeks later my father and a few of the other higher-ups came down to the warehouse to address the workers. We made sure not to make eye contact. Pointing to my father, Suni nudged me.

"He's a Canadian," she said.

"One of those," I responded.

My father and the rest of the guys in ties stood against the back wall of the warehouse. All the workers left their stations and gathered around.

"First off, I would just like to say thank you for all the hard work," my dad said.

The workers looked at each other and smiled. I antici-pated my dad was going to follow up with some bad news. Whenever someone thanks you for all your hard work, it's usually followed with a "but we're going to have to let you go" or "no more bagel Fridays at the end of the month."

"We've got a tight deadline coming up and I'm going to have to implement mandatory overtime this week."

I was right—bad news.

"Damn, overtime, this sucks," I said to Jerry, after my dad and the rest of the higher-ups went back upstairs to their offices.

"This is good. More money," he responded.

"Money, money, money," Suni sang, rotating her arms doing an awkward version of the cabbage patch. "Time and a half!"

The first week of overtime was a complete one-eighty compared to my life in college. My five-class schedule and occasional odd job took twenty-five hours of my whole week. I chose how to spend the remaining time. Fifty hours of responsibility over five straight days was a drastic change. I was so exhausted that when I got home on Friday and my dad offered to take me to the beach for a surf lesson, I declined.

By the second week I adapted to the schedule and looked forward to the final two hours of the day because we were allowed to listen to the radio. Ranchera music overpowered the industrial hum that filled the space around my head during regular hours, putting me and everyone else in a positive mood.

"I can use this money to get my daughter those piano lessons she's been asking for," Suni said as she bobbed her head to the music.

"My son wants a skateboard," Jerry said. "We'll see what's left over after all the bills."

"Bills are no fun," Suni said.

"Okay. Disneyland with the family!"

"You're crazy, Yeddy!"

"How about you Steven? What will you spend the extra money on?"

"It's going straight into savings for school."

"Good boy," she said. A new song came on the radio and she bobbed her head to the music. "Dance with me." She grabbed my hand and raised it in the air and spun herself under it.

At the end of the week I felt rich. I'd never seen a paycheck that big with my name on it. It was nice to see my hard work boiled down to dollars and cents. Until that point my money had been going straight into my savings account reserved for books, pizza, and weed when I returned to college. I treated myself to a couple of Wu-Tang CDs and Bukowski's *Factotum*.

On my last day Suni asked me where I went for lunch. I brought a sandwich every day, and even though I could have eaten in the cafeteria, I felt more comfortable sitting in my car alone with a book. I had enough trouble making small talk on the line. I found it easiest to drive two blocks down the road and eat in an empty parking lot while reading Alex Garland's *The Beach*. The quiet time I spent lost in the story of a guy my age living life on a secluded island filled with marijuana plants was the perfect escape after four hours of robotic work. I had to set an alarm to alert myself when it was time to head back. Otherwise, I'd get so engulfed in the story I'd forget to return to my station.

"I read a book in my car," I said.

"That's sad. Eat with us in the cafeteria," she said. "Meals should be shared with friends."

The cafeteria was segregated into line workers, supervisors, tech support, and maintenance crew, which were then segregated into race. I sat with Jerry and Suni at the Filipino table with my PB&J.

"Speak English," Suni said to the table as I sat down.

The table went quiet. Everyone stared into their Tupperware containers filled with rice and noodles in strange-colored sauces. One woman, who I'd never seen before, was spooning fist-sized spoonfuls of rice and beans in her mouth when she stopped and smiled at me.

"You're so handsome," she said. "Maybe I introduce you to my niece sometime."

"Okay," I said opening my sandwich bag revealing the familiar smell of peanut butter.

"Steven, you should try Yeddy's balut," Suni said.

"He won't like it," Jerry said.

"What is it?"

Jerry pushed a container in front of me and handed me a plastic fork. I glimpsed what looked like a hard-boiled egg, buried under grayish-brown stuff mixed with brown rice.

"He's not going to eat it," Suni said.

"I'll try it," I said. I'm not an adventurous eater. Growing up I spent most family dinners pushing my mother's meatloaf or baked chicken around the plate, negotiating how many bites I had to take before I could just have Honey Nut Cheerios instead.

I cut off a small piece and brought it to my mouth. The fleshy glob dangled off the fork and smelled like spoiled shellfish. I placed it on my tongue and slowly moved it around my mouth afraid to bite down. It was slimy. Suni stared at my mouth anticipating that I would spit it out. It slid into the back of my throat. Suni gave me an encouraging head nod. I swallowed.

"You like?" Suni asked.

"It's good," I lied. It tasted like Silly Putty soaked in vinegar, but still better than raw pig parts stuffed into a PB&J, I imagined. I took a huge swig of my water to rinse my mouth.

"White boys usually don't like balut," Jerry said.

"Most white boys wouldn't even try balut," Suni said.

Jerry told me about growing up in a Filipino village that sometimes struggled to get clean water. At age twenty-two he'd saved enough money to move to America. He sent part of his paycheck back to his brother, who he hoped would join him in California when he got a visa. I was about to tell him that I was here with a green card, but quickly remembered that Steven Barton was American. It was disappointing that I couldn't reveal that I was a fellow foreigner. Our coming-to-America stories were different, but we still shared the bond of being immigrants.

"Back to school," Suni said toward the end of the day.

"You were fun to work with," I said.

It wasn't the beach summer I had hoped for. I didn't play volleyball with any beach babes, but the time I spent with Suni and Jerry made the job a positive experience. Yet at the end of the two months I was ready to move on.

I was excited to get back on campus, fix my own schedule, and not be attached to a power drill. I craved the free time to read and have three-hour conversations on the underlying themes of loneliness and alienation in Hemingway's work. Or sleep until noon simply because I felt like it.

"Will you eat balut when you get back to school?" Suni asked.

"They don't serve it in the cafeteria. Maybe if I go to the international part of town. I bet they'd be impressed to see a white boy like me order balut."

"Bring a girl. She'll think you're very exotic," she said, laughing.

On the last day of August, I loaded my things into the back of my dad's car. The weather was perfect, just the same as the day he picked me up, as well as every day in between. Before I headed into the airport, my dad pulled a crisp hundred-dollar bill from his money clip and handed it to me. "Fold this up and put it behind your license in your wallet."

"Thanks, but for what?"

"An emergency," he said. "I missed out on a lot of fun when I was in college because I was always broke. Have some of the fun I missed."

•

A few years later I was sitting in a cubicle drinking coffee and fighting with a spreadsheet. I was late on a deadline because I couldn't figure out how to place a pie chart in the top left corner of the page. I looked up at the corkboard ceiling and calmed myself with a deep breath. I closed my eyes and remembered those repetitive days as Steven Barton. I missed the mindlessness of the work. I had a clearly defined task that I worked at until 3:30, and when I clocked out, my concerns about fans and hard drives disappeared until I returned the next day. I'd lost that feeling. Work was always on my mind. "Do I have a meeting tomorrow? Shit, I have to have that completed by noon. Man, I hate that jerk-off Bradley."

I never thought like that at the warehouse. There'd always be more fans to drill, and that was that, which made it possible for Suni and Jerry to provide for their families, which in turn allowed my father to provide for his.

I noticed the drone of keyboard chatter for the first time that day and looked over at the girl across the aisle. She wore earphones and stared intently at her computer screen. We had traded smiles every morning and afternoon for the past three months. The only thing I knew about her was that she liked strawberry yogurt and was environmentally conscious enough to reuse the same plastic spoon for weeks at a time. I didn't know if she had a daughter who wanted to learn piano or if she dreamed of one day taking her family to Disneyland. Had her name not been written on her cubicle wall I'm not even sure I'd have known it was Angela.

I never saw Suni or Jerry again after my final day. I believed they were both on the assembly line at that exact moment, chatting about their families while installing fans. Suni was probably nervously laughing after something she just said.

I stood up from my desk to fill up my coffee mug. As I passed by the girl in the cubicle I lingered for just a moment, hoping she might stop me and ask for a dance.

The Jump (It's Only Temporary)

I kept my beer in my hand, never putting it down for fear of picking up the wrong one and drinking in a mouthful of ash and cigarette butts. A barefooted blonde sat across from me and puffed on a joint that popped every time the cherry burned through a seed.

It was a Tuesday night. I'd just gotten off work and was sitting on the couch in the living room of The Club House, a four-room crash pad in Ocean Beach that my buddy Daniel shared with a revolving door of tenants. It was supposed to be a low-key night, not like Friday or Saturday when we drank until the house was dry or the sun rose.

Daniel was a junior studying business at San Diego State; he still had time to make mistakes and run up his parents' credit card without ever seeing a bill. I was a twenty-two-year-old recent college graduate staying with my parents rent-free for the summer. I was building my savings before moving to Seattle in the fall.

I had a temp job picking and shipping in a medical supply warehouse. After work my mom cooked me dinner and I drank my father's beers. Sometimes we played cards, and other nights I sat in the guest room watching HBO.

I spent weekends at The Club House, where I showed up Friday after work and didn't leave until Sunday afternoon. I slept on the couch or on an oversize beanbag. One night I tried to steal Daniel's bed, but I got out when he stripped off all his clothes and hopped in next to me and asked if I wanted to be the little spoon.

We'd known each other since we were kids living on the East Coast. I was close with his whole family and hung out in their kitchen after school and rummaged through their fridge. His older brother and I used to sneak cigarettes in the woods. I was happy to spend the summer living with my parents because I knew I could go to The Club House and live like I was still in college.

My girlfriend, Ashley, who was moving to Seattle with me, was on the East Coast for the summer. In August we'd drive up together, then rent an apartment, and I'd start my career. I felt like cohabitation and a full-time job were things expected of me after I received my degree.

Before Ashley went back east, my father pulled me aside and offered to get her a job at his company, so she could live with us for the summer. I never mentioned that opportunity to her. I wanted one last independent experience before we combined our lives into a one-bedroom apartment.

"I've got to be up early for work tomorrow," I said.

"Work is lame," Daniel said.

The blonde passed me the joint. The paper crackled as I inhaled. When I handed it back, she smiled, revealing a gap in her front teeth.

I liked talking with the California stoner chicks that hung around The Club House, and they seemed to like me. It never went past playful flirting, but sometimes I felt guilty.

"Hey guys," we heard Todd say before he entered the room. He turned the corner, and I saw that he was wearing his CHICKS DIG ME trucker hat, which he only put on after eight beers. Most of the time he was a Dean's List student and captain of the lacrosse team, but after sucking down a few beers, it was impossible to know he was on track to becoming a big shot in the financial world. "Want to jump off a bridge?"

"Are you serious?" Daniel asked.

"Yeah, it's about fifty feet above the jetty."

"Is it safe?"

"I don't think anyone's died," Todd said. "It will get your adrenaline pumping. Take a risk."

"I'm in," I said.

I liked the guys I worked with at the warehouse even though I didn't feel like one of them. They wore steel-toed boots and pants with double-stitched knees while I worked in cargo shorts and sneakers. They drove pickup trucks with cracked side view mirrors and had banged-up lunch boxes with matching thermoses filled with black coffee. They compared this warehouse to others they worked at—which one had the hottest women working the front desk and which one had the best vending machines. They smoked cigarette brands I'd never heard of that smelled like charcoal. Their children were always getting detention, and their ex-wives slept around. They spent weekends in casinos and strip clubs and always tried to get me to tag along. They thought I was crazy when I said strip clubs made me uncomfortable and casinos were a waste of money.

One day a man in a tie who worked in the air-conditioned office above the warehouse needed help loading boxes into his car. He asked me if I was in school, and I told him I had just graduated.

"Then why are you here?" he asked.

He was relieved when I told him it was only temporary.

One Sunday afternoon I was driving home from The Club House while I pounded Gatorade to cure my hangover. There was an accident on the highway, and traffic was stalled. I was dehydrated, and combined with the Monday's-coming doldrums, my anxiety about the move revealed itself. I'd been suppressing my doubt since Ashley left, but as the car in front of me came to a full stop, I worried I wasn't ready to live with someone and get a job that required a degree and forty hours a week.

What I really wanted to do was write, which had been a hobby until sophomore year of college when I read Brett Easton Ellis's *Less Than Zero*. It was the first book I read and thought *I could do that*. Paying bills as a novelist seemed much more fulfilling than working in an office, but I never shared those thoughts with anyone. It was basically like telling someone I wanted to be an astronaut. "Oh, that's cute, but when that doesn't pan out, what would you actually like to do?" I assumed people would say.

I couldn't image going to the same office every day for the next forty years of my life. My father was happy working sixty hours a week and spending half the year on business trips because it gave him satisfaction to know his hard work gave me opportunities he never had. I didn't plan on having kids because I didn't want someone depending on me for opportunities. I'd rather focus on making my own.

I knew I should have already been in my car headed home as the four of us walked down an unlit bike path. Daniel passed me a bottle of tequila.

"Work's going to be rough tomorrow," I said after taking a swig that caused me to shiver.

"I have to work for two hours tomorrow," Daniel responded.

"You mean sit at a desk and surf the web?" I said as a joint found its way to my lips. I took a sweet hit that made the back of my throat numb.

"Don't knock my internship, man. It's going to land me a job after I graduate."

"Too early to worry about that," I said.

"That's the type of attitude that lands a college graduate living with his parents and working in a warehouse." He pulled the joint from my hand, causing a dustup of orange embers that evaporated in the breeze.

"It's just for the money," I said. "This is my last hurrah in blue collar work."

"Are you going home soon?" the blonde asked. I looked at her as we passed a faraway house with its porch light on and caught a glimpse of her face and the gap in her teeth. "You should stay longer," she said.

"I have to work tomorrow, but we'll see."

The idea to move to Seattle came about after a drunken phone conversation with a college buddy who'd moved there a year prior. After graduation all my friends had left town and started careers while I was still living in the same apartment and working the same job delivering flowers. I was in need of a change and was sold on Seattle when my friend offered up his guestroom and Ashley said she'd go with me.

Since I planned on moving in the fall, I wasn't picky when seeking out a summer job. I told the woman at the staffing agency I was looking for something short-term. I was presented with a few options and took a warehouse position because it was a mile from my parents' house. I didn't even have to get on the highway for the commute, and I could go home for lunch, but mainly I ate in the parking lot with Joey. He was my age and had a kid and an ex-wife.

We spent the day loading and unloading trucks. When there weren't any trucks, Joey and I pushed brooms through the stacks of boxes. We talked about movies, or he would tell me about crimes he committed growing up in the Philippines. Before moving to the States, he robbed tourists and broke into cars to support his younger brothers and sisters.

•

We lined up on the side of the bridge farthest from the streetlight. I had to trust Todd that we were above water because all I could see below was darkness. A car drove past and lit up our group. The blonde's hair had fallen across her face, and she nervously bit down on her thumb.

When the car's light faded, we hopped over the railing and dangled our feet off the bridge. It was quiet, and as I looked out into the distance, unable to tell where the water and the night sky met, I felt like I was exactly where I should be.

Todd broke the silence with a cheer and leaped off the bridge. There was a splash, and I held my breath until I heard him emerge from the water.

"Who's next?" he called up to us.

Daniel looked at me as he leaned off the bridge. "See ya on the flip side," he said as his body spilled into the unknown.

The blonde intermingled her fingers with mine. I assumed she was a classmate of Daniel's, but I didn't know. I wondered who she was and what motivated her to get wasted on a Tuesday night. I looked down at her delicate fingers threaded with mine and thought about Ashley.

"I'm nervous too," I whispered.

"Come on, jerks!" Daniel yelled up to us.

The blonde and I jumped off the bridge. Our fingers slipped from each other's hands, and I hung in the air long enough to see Daniel and Todd pass the bottle between them.

I crashed into the water. The deeper I sank, the colder I got. I kept expecting to hit bottom, but I never did. I pulled myself back to the surface and heard Daniel and Todd cheering. I swam to the shore with the blonde trailing behind me.

"That was rad," she said.

We walked back to Daniel's while dripping wet and passing around the bottle of tequila, now covered in sand and almost empty. The saltwater on my lips made it go down easier than before.

"I'm going to skip my internship tomorrow," Daniel said. "We should go to Del Mar and play the ponies."

"I'm in," I said.

Daniel and I spent the rest of the night drinking beers and listening to music on his porch. The blonde slept on the beanbag and was gone by the time we went inside for scrambled eggs.

Without sleeping or changing our clothes, we jumped in Daniel's car and drove to the racetrack. We sipped mojitos and made five-dollar show bets that never paid out. We were having too much fun to feel like we were losing money. We picked horses with funny names and cheered them on with over-the-top enthusiasm, even when they were trailing by half a lap.

The next day I walked into work feeling guilty that my absence had caused extra work for Joey, but I didn't regret my decision to skip. The smaller paycheck was worth the experience, and I was confident Joey had no trouble picking up my slack. He was twice the worker I was because, unlike me, the job was more than money. He was gaining experience that he could take to the next warehouse that hired him, and he believed that hard work eventually resulted in financial stability, which would provide his child opportunities he never had growing up in the Philippines.

Joey and I had been hired as equals, but he took the lead when organizing the best way to load each truck. He wasn't dominating, and I was happy to take orders. It was obvious he knew more than I did. When I told him I wasn't comfortable loading boxes with the forklift because I'd never done it before, he taught me.

"Knowing how to drive one of these can add an extra two bucks an hour to your paycheck," he said as I reversed the forklift out of the truck after successfully loading a pallet weighing over three hundred pounds

"Cool," I said without mentioning that, once I moved to Seattle, I didn't plan on working in a warehouse ever again.

Before I had a chance to get to my manager's office to lie about my absence, Joey stopped me. "Don't sweat it," he said and slapped me on the shoulder. "I covered for you."

"Thanks," I said.

It was possible that, without Joey's help, my manager would have given me a strike and I would have been able to keep my job, but I was grateful that he stepped up for me. He was a friend.

Two months later Ashley and I were in my car with the backseat and trunk packed with our stuff. We had donated our dishware and furniture to Goodwill with the intention of buying new stuff in Seattle. We'd replace my chipped plates that had traveled between dorm rooms and studio apartments with something more adult, and buy a coffee table that didn't have "420" carved into the edge.

We listened to mix CDs loaded with grunge songs that had themes of apathy and angst, which we had created specifically for the trip. Ashley talked about getting a dog once we were settled. I thought about the money I had saved and wondered how long twelve hundred bucks would last in Seattle. We drove through the night, and I kept one hand on the wheel and linked my free hand with hers. "I'm nervous too," I said while driving deeper into darkness, unsure where the sky and highway met.

"So, you're just going to be like this forever?"

It was the only job I ever had where I could masturbate on the clock without fear of committing a serious HR violation. My work outfit was a pair of mesh shorts and a tank top. Flannel bottoms and a hoodie on cold days. I made my own coffee and never had to write my name on the half and half I kept in the fridge. My commute was shorter than the average playground hopscotch grid.

I was an off-site content writer for Expedia.com, hired through an agency for a six-month contract with the possibility of an extension based on performance. After a string of office jobs that required no previous skills, I felt like I was finally working a job where my English degree was an asset.

Content writer—a title alone that offered me a sense of pride I had never felt as an office gofer. When I ran into someone from high school and they asked me what I was up to I could say, "I'm a content writer."

My first day was on-site. I was put in the care of Jane, a senior content writer and my main contact for questions and assignments. A Cartman doll sat on top of her computer monitor, and she had a split keyboard designed to be ergonomic. Having only ever used regular keyboards, I found it intimidating. Jane pointed me to an Excel spreadsheet that had a list of amenities for a Howard Johnson's in Bakersfield, California, and told me to turn the list into complete sentences.

I pecked at the unfamiliar keyboard and took five minutes to write "Free High-Speed internet." She pointed out that "Internet" is supposed to be capitalized—a grammar rule I was aware of but chose not to follow. I guess you can argue "The Internet" is a destination, but something about that capital "I" made me uncomfortable. Jane excused herself to get coffee and said she'd return in fifteen minutes to check on my progress.

I crafted an elegant room description about fluffy pillows to rest your head on after a long drive, and towels so soft you'll want to wear them as pajamas. Jane wasn't impressed.

"Cut all descriptive words," she said. "You have no idea if those pillows are fluffy. Stick with the basics. Instead of saying 'soft towels,' just say 'towels.'"

I was relieved that I wouldn't have to spend my days flipping through a thesaurus looking for different ways to say "comfortable." At the same time, part of me was disappointed that I wouldn't have the opportunity for poetry.

I spent the rest of the day at Jane's desk under the watchful eye of her Cartman doll. Occasionally, she popped her head in to check on my work. She was gracious with her critiques, and by the end of the day, I had the basic skills required to be a content writer for Expedia. She assigned me a laptop, and I was on my way.

When I got home that night Ashley was sitting at the computer working on a paper for class. She had traded her work clothes for shorts and one of my hoodies. I walked up behind her and moved her blonde hair to the side and kissed her neck.

"I'm a motherfucking content writer," I said.

She smiled at me like she had twenty-four hours into our first date, when she woke me up wearing my Beatles T-shirt and handed me a mug of coffee. It was the smile I learned to recognize as meaning everything was okay.

The job meant we could move out of our damp-smelling one-bedroom basement apartment with a shower that filled up past our ankles no matter how much Drano we poured down it.

Ashley had been the breadwinner of the relationship. Within two weeks of our arrival in Seattle, she had registered for school and acquired a full-time job at a local hospital. I spent the first two weeks drinking Carlo Rossi and writing Bukowski-inspired poetry. Before moving into the basement apartment, we stayed in our friend Brian's guest room. While she was at work, Brian and I smoked joints and brainstormed ideas for chapbooks and literary events.

It wasn't long before Ashley got sick of returning home from a full day of work to find me unshowered and blurry-eyed, with nothing to show for the day except a few scribbled poems written on the inside flap of a beer box.

Brian and I met in a poetry workshop in college and shared postgrad aspirations that focused more on getting our writing out into the world than securing stable employ-ment. We spent whole days in his living room putting together chapbooks with titles like *Unemployed College Grads* and *Unemployed Stoners and Full-Time Drunks*.

At night we checked out literary readings around the city and often found them boring, usually leaving early to grab a drink. The audience seemed like it was a chore for them to be there and only attended so the following day they could tell their coworkers they went to a poetry read-ing, which would make them feel like good art patrons. Brian and I wanted to come up with a reading that people were excited about, instead of a crowd of liberal-leaning capitalists who supported the arts to relieve some of their upper-middle-class guilt.

Ashley only saw it as going out to bars and waking the next day with a hangover. She didn't believe that what I called "research" was anything more than getting drunk. She doubted I'd ever take initiative to move out of the guest room. It was valid reasoning, because I barely browsed the help-wanted section.

"As soon as I get a job, we'll look for a place," I said to her in the middle of the night. Our legs were intertwined, and my ass hung off the twin bed we shared in the guest room. It was rare for us to find comfort at the same time. I never reached full REM until after 6:00 a.m. when she got up to shower before work.

I stared at a poster of Method Man and Red Man with peeling corners that hung above the bed. They were each holding brightly colored bottles of St. Ides and had devious grins, as if they were just about to start one of those nights when the only thing remembered the next morning was that it was fucking fun. It used to hang in Brian's college apartment, and I remembered staring at it when we'd blow off our biology lab to smoke and listen to underground rap records. When he and his girlfriend moved into the house, she refused to allow it in the living room.

I tried to roll over and accidentally kneed Ashley in the back.

"We have to move," she said. "I'll pay deposit and first and last month's rent."

We moved into a one-bedroom apartment in Capitol Hill, and I got a job delivering pizza. I liked it because working nights allowed me to write during the day, and business was so slow I spent most of my shift talking hockey with the cook.

Unfortunately, business was so slow it eventually shut down. I might have never quit had I not been forced out.

The fourteen bucks an hour I would earn as a content writer was enough to ease Ashley's fear that she'd have to support me for the rest of our lives. We celebrated by splitting six taquitos and three margarita pitchers at our favorite Mexican restaurant.

The following morning I woke at 6:30 a.m. to the alarm on Ashley's side of the bed. She popped up and went into the shower like she'd been doing every morning since we moved in. I fished my slippers off the carpet and put them on while still under the covers. Even though I'd yet to look out the window, I knew it was raining. Ashley put on her works clothes, then donned rain boots and a jacket. She pulled the umbrella from the closet and was out the door.

I put on a pair of flannel pajama bottoms and an oversize hoodie.

Jane had already sent me a spreadsheet of the day's assignments. I had seventy-five hotels that needed descriptions, and when I was finished with those, I was to ask for more. I wrote my first description, then compared it to my notes from the previous day's training session to make sure I followed the style guide correctly. I clicked spell-check a few times even though no words had been marked with a jagged red underline. I reread the description for a third time and hit publish.

I opened Expedia.com to view my work, my biggest publication to date. I had a few poems published and wrote for my college newspaper, but this had a potential audience of millions.

Wireless Internet access (surcharge) keeps you connected, and satellite channels are offered for your entertainment. Request an in-room massage. Shower/tub combination in the private bathroom, as well as a hair dryer. Air-conditioning, a safe, and a desk are among the conveniences offered. No smoking.

It was a change from the drunken and anxiety-themed prose poetry I usually wrote, but it paid better.

I don't like one-hour lunch breaks because it's more time than necessary to consume a turkey sandwich and a bottle of water. I prefer a short break that results in early dismissal.

However, when working from home, a free midday hour is an opportunity to take care of errands that feel tedious when squeezed between the valuable hours between the office and home.

It's always Black Friday at the grocery store after 5:00 p.m., but instead of discount TVs, people are fighting to maximize their time on leave from the office. Midday had a whole different vibe. No one rushed between the beer aisle and the frozen pizza section. People had the patience to squeeze avocados until they found one that was soft, but not too soft, and no one cut in line at the deli counter.

I took my time picking out all the ingredients to bake a lasagna—the only meal I learned to prepare in college that didn't involve a microwave. It had been a while since I'd made it, because I never had the patience for the line at the cheese counter after a day in the office.

I listened to NPR as I baked the lasagna once, let it cool, then put it in the fridge to bake a second time when Ashley returned home. After years perfecting my recipe, I discovered that lasagna tastes best after a second bake, which was my preferred method, but I rarely had the time.

Ashley returned home wet and exhausted to a warm apartment filled with the smell of roasting garlic and basil. She peeled off of her work clothes and changed into jeans and my hoodie, which had become hers.

"Any wine to go with the meal?" she asked while pulling her hair back into a ponytail.

"No, but I can get some. Feel like drinking?" I asked.

"Duh," she said and then shook her hips. "It's been a long day."

Ashley and I had each fallen in love with alcohol before falling in love with each other, and together we were marathon drinkers. We unconsciously egged the other on so as not to feel insecure about our own overindulgence. I knew she was the one for me after she drank me under the table going shot for shot with Jäger and then washed my sheets the next day because I'd pissed the bed.

My dating history was exclusively drinkers, but she was the only one who also followed the practices of absolving every bender with exercise. We once spent a month in Sydney, Australia, where we stumbled home from the bar every single night and woke every morning to a run around the harbor.

Ashley made exaggerated "mmm" sounds with every bite of the lasagna and was happy that there would be leftovers she could take to work. When we were done eating, we put on Fleetwood Mac's *Rumours* instead of turning on the TV, which had become our after-dinner routine over the past few weeks. We opened another bottle of wine, and she sat on my lap as we researched apartments to visit over the weekend.

The following day's hangover was easy to manage working from home. I drank Gatorade and ate buttered bagels and went for a run on my lunch break. Unlike being hungover at the office, I never once wished for death. I didn't experience the heart-pounding anxiety that comes when talking to a coworker while knowing I have booze on my breath. And I certainly didn't miss the nervous sweats that soaked through my shirt while I counted down the hours before I could go home and hide myself in bed.

Once I figured out the formula to writing room descriptions for Expedia, the job felt more like data entry than writing. The difference between a Best Western in Seattle and a Best Western in Miami was so minimal that I could reuse the same description with only minor changes. Most rooms only took a few minutes to write. Sometimes I was assigned a unique room in a bed and breakfast with only a few blurry photos as my guide and spent twenty minutes trying to determine if the bathtub was claw-footed or not. But excluding the occasional problem location, I could complete sixty-five to seventy-five rooms a day, which seemed to satisfy Jane. Days went by when we didn't speak. She only contacted me when I made a mistake.

Steven, I just got an email from the property manager of the La Quinta Inn in Rochester, New York. He's upset because you forgot to mention the rooms are equipped with complimentary shampoo and conditioner.

I turned off the talk radio and pasted "complimentary shampoo and conditioner" into fourteen room descriptions.

Jane, so sorry for the mistake. I promise to be more careful. All updates complete!

Knowing what I needed to do to keep Jane happy allowed me to shift from working an hourly schedule to a room-count quota. I didn't consider it devious—had I been in the office I would have spent at least two hours a day surfing the web or hiding in the bathroom.

I completed forty to fifty rooms in the morning between loads of laundry and cleaning up around the apartment. At noon I'd go for a run and then eat a Lean Pocket while watching a rerun of *Rosanne*. I posted the remaining rooms throughout the day, while I took breaks to write or read, making sure my messenger status was always available.

Ashley worked forty hours a week and was a full-time student. By the time she'd completed a day of work, sat through a couple of lectures, and walked the mile and half back to our apartment, I was halfway through a bottle of wine and tinkering with a poem.

"Can I read you this thing I wrote?" I asked before she even had a chance to take off her jacket.

"Can you give me a minute?"

"Of course. There's wine on the counter if you want it."

"Great," she said in a tone that was neither enthusiastic nor sarcastic, but heavyhearted enough to let me know she was not pleased.

I stared at my computer and crinkled my brow to seem as though I was contemplating a word. She glared at me as she filled her glass and didn't notice when it spilled over the side.

"Shit," she said and pulled open the drawer with such force the rattle of the cutlery startled me. "So, you've just been drinking wine all night?"

"I've been writing too," I said while trying to sound as though the half bottle of wine I drank was excusable because I also completed a poem. "How was your day?"

"Shitty."

"That sucks. Have a glass of wine. Maybe you'll feel better."

Once she had a buzz going, she would return to the girl who liked hanging out with me. We'd sit across from each other at the dinner table typing away at our laptops, stopping every once in a while to share a line. Each of us trusted the other's opinion and said encouraging things like, "I really like the image you used there" or "that metaphor pops off the page." Those were the moments that reminded me why I didn't want to be with anyone else. It was reminiscent of our first year together, before moving to Seattle. When no world existed outside ourselves.

One morning we were running along the beach, and we both started laughing as we passed a Rollerblade cop. We each had the exact same thought—all a criminal needed to do to get away was run on the sand.

It sparked an idea and we spent the night creating a comic about Ronny the Rollerblade Cop and his misadventures chasing dope smokers in Huntington Beach. Ashley did the illustrations, and we collaborated on writing situations that resulted in Ronny failing to stop a crime because his blades couldn't go on sand. Our minds were so in sync that, when the sun came up, we had completed a whole sketchbook's worth of comics.

Once we ate mushrooms and concluded that we shared a creative conscious that we called *Quim* and believed we were connected on a spiritual level that allowed us to communicate on a frequency outside of ourselves. It made all the uncertainties of the universe irrelevant because our

51

bond was our version of god. Even after the psilocybin wore off, we continued calling our creative collaborations Quim.

All that died down when we moved to Seattle. Our responsibilities didn't allow us to pull all-nighters just because we came up with a good idea. Most nights after dinner, we'd play a board game and then fall asleep watching a crime drama. Eventually, we stopped making art as a team and Quim just became an easy way to get rid of a "Q" in Scrabble.

I found a routine with work that provided me time to write and waste whole afternoons sitting on a bar stool next to Brian. We were planning art events, so it felt like more than just hanging out at a bar. The job allowed me to make my own schedule, as long as I met expectations, and I had the benefit of not having to waste half my day commuting. I never worried about staying out too late on weeknights because I could always work in bed if I was too tired to sit at my desk.

While Ashley was at evening classes, I was organizing literary events, collaborating on a chapbook, or scouting the city for poets to invite to my series. It was easy to understand why she would be envious of my schedule, but I never tried hard enough to understand why it angered her.

Ashley had developed a strong work ethic early in life. Her parents were young and never married. Unlike my childhood, where my biggest concern was how much candy I could get with my five-dollar allowance, she was working odd jobs to help out her single mother and three younger half-brothers. When she was fourteen she worked at the local Baskin-Robbins after school and on weekends. Her forearms were so strong from scooping ice cream, she could beat all the boys in her class at arm wrestling.

After a year in the new apartment, Ashley wanted more. She'd graduated college and found a job that she enjoyed and paid well. The graffiti on the side of our building and the shoes hanging from the telephone wire had lost their charm. She wanted a house we could call our own, with weekend projects like digging out a garden or painting a fence—a place where we could have a dog and a backyard. She wanted what she never had as a kid.

"Don't you want something better than this?" she asked one night when the episode of *Top Chef* we were watching was interrupted by a couple shouting below our window.

"I think they're arguing about drugs," I said.

"They're always arguing about drugs. I'm sick of it."

"I think she's pissed because he didn't share his last rock."

Ashley clicked the remote, muting the TV. She put her hand on my lap and waited for me to face her. "I want us to buy a house," she said.

I held my eyes shut while I tried to think of a way to change the subject. We had had this conversation before, and it was becoming harder to avoid. Buying a house was a long-term contract I wasn't prepared to sign. I was satisfied with our relationship, but I was aware that since moving to Seattle, we had slowly been drifting apart. I was content in the moment, but I couldn't predict how I'd feel five years in the future.

53

"I just don't think I'm ready," I said.

"Why?"

I wasn't brave enough to tell her the truth and instead chose a different excuse as to why I couldn't commit. "What happens if my job ends and I can't pay the mortgage?"

"Have you ever thought of looking for another job?"

"But I like my job."

"You like worrying every six months? You're always a wreck the days leading up to your contract extension date."

"Thankfully, it always gets renewed," I said.

A frustrated wrinkle split her forehead. "What's your plan then? You're just going to continue working this job until one day they don't extend you? Then what?"

"I guess I'll look for another job. But the time off will be great for writing. I could finally start my novel."

"That's it then?"

"What's it?"

"You don't want to buy a house with me?"

"I do." Her eyes were locked with mine, and I knew if I looked away she'd close herself in the bedroom and I'd be sleeping on the couch. It was a look I'd become more accustomed to than that smile I first saw in my Beatles T-shirt. "Just not right now."

"When?"

"Aren't you happy?" I motioned with my arms to display the fruits of our apartment as if I was a *Price Is Right* model and Ashley was bidding on our life.

I broke eye contact for a second to see who would be named winner of the Quick Fire Challenge. A pebble-size puddle formed in the corner of her eye. She blinked, and a tear dripped down her cheek.

"So, you're just going to be like this forever?"

She waited for an answer and when it didn't come she went into the bedroom and closed the door. I heard her sobbing into a pillow.

Once every six months I was called into the office for a training session. A person I only knew as an email address would teach me a new program or show me a change to the style guide. It was usually something simple that I could have learned over the phone, but I assumed they brought me in to make sure I was still alive.

I became so comfortable with the digital relationship I shared with my coworkers that I almost forgot each email address was attached to an actual human. I was brought in for a meeting by my supervisor, who I knew by the email handle "Phitten," and I half expected to spend the day with an adorable little cat.

"Good morning, Steven," she said when we met in the lobby. She was tall and confident and didn't possess any feline features.

I was dressed in my most professional-looking work shirt, which Ashley had ironed the night before after I found it in the back of the closet, flattened under a suitcase.

"We're on the tenth floor," she said as the elevator doors closed behind us.

"That's nice," I said while looking down at the dress shoes that my mom insisted on buying me the week before I graduated college, when I told her I planned on walking in sneakers. I was trying to calculate if I'd worn them enough to justify the $150 price tag while I waited for Phitten to fill the silence. I anticipated a conversational quip about the weather or the traffic, but the silence lingered and hovered above us, until she reached across me and pressed ten on the keypad.

"Sorry," I said and realized she'd been waiting for me to hit the button.

"It's okay," she said and looked down at the ground. I wondered if she was looking at my shoes and if they looked as she expected. My randomly generated handle was "Stbark," which I verbalized as "Saint Bark." Had she been expecting some sort of saint-like dog? Or maybe a Saint Bernard named "Bark"?

For the next three hours she demonstrated a program that searched hotel amenity content. I took notes I knew I'd never look at because I wanted her to think our time was worthwhile. I was already familiar with the tool, but revealing that I didn't require training would force her to find another way to validate the time, which meant teaching me a new skill. Temping taught me to keep watch for responsibilities outside of the job description. Unless it came with a pay raise or a full-time position, it wasn't worth my time.

We were reviewing different types of spreadsheet formatting when "Sytana" stopped by. I was disappointed he wasn't a seventy-year-old psychedelic guitar hero like I'd imagined every time I received an email from him.

"Hey, Steve," he said. "You decided to put pants on and come to the office, did ya?"

"Yeah."

"I'm just kidding with you. How ya been?"

"Good," I said.

"All right, see ya around, bud." He slapped the door frame and continued down the hall.

When Phitten walked me out of the office at the end of the day, we passed a whiteboard that said, "Margarita cupcake happy hour at 5:00!"

"You can stick around," she said.

"Thanks," I said. "But I've got my buddy's kid tonight."

Ashley left for a week to visit her family back east, and for the first time in a while it was easier to breathe. The walls of the apartment had been closing in on us. The only place we found comfort was on opposite sides of the couch, facing the TV. Hours went by without so much as a glance in the other's direction, and the silence only broke when one asked the other what to watch next.

Having stocked up on food and beer the day she left, I savored the solitude. By day three, I couldn't remember the last time I'd spoken out loud. "Woo," I said under my breath, testing to see if I could still speak. "Woo, woo," I said again. "Heeey, Macarena." Once I established that my voice still worked, I started talking to myself as I moved around the apartment. "How about a beer?" I said as I reached into the fridge. "Don't mind if I do."

57

I spent the night sitting on the carpet flipping through a journal Ashley and I used to share. I read poems we'd written together back when buying a house was not a concern and we never disagreed.

Ashley's trip home reminded her how much she missed her family. Her brothers loved when she visited because she took them out to dinner and bought them new clothes. They had grown up depending on her, and when she moved across the country, they felt abandoned.

"Do you ever think about moving back east?" she asked one night when we were lying in bed.

"No."

"I do. My brothers need me."

"That's why it's good to visit."

"I worry about them sometimes."

I rolled over and faced the wall.

By my third year at Expedia I'd stopped feeling like a temp. As far as I knew I had a full-time job and stopped concerning myself whenever I was up for an extension. I assumed as long as I continued doing what I'd been doing, my job was secure, which was a similar approach I applied to the relationship, though with less success.

Outside of work I focused on writing and various projects I was putting together with Brian, while Ashley found a renewed passion for dance. She'd done it her whole life, until we got together and it took a backseat to writing. Her interest returned after taking a hip-hop class with a coworker. She joined a team that competed locally and spent her nights working on routines. The more she became involved in the lifestyle, the less interest she had in drinking, which made it difficult for her to live with someone who was constantly coming home drunk.

"Why do you need another beer?" she asked when I returned home from a reading and pulled a beer from the back of the fridge.

"Why not?" I responded.

"Because you're already drunk."

"What's the problem with one more?"

"Whatever, I'm going to bed," she said.

She closed the door to the bedroom, and I drank the last three beers in the fridge and wrote a poem that I never looked at again.

A few nights later I came home after spending four hours with Brian and a few writer friends in a bar. We were planning the fourth season of our reading series called "Cheap Wine & Poetry." We sold wine for five bucks a bottle and featured the hottest readers in Seattle. The place was packed every night. Ashley had come in the beginning, but grew tired of waking up the next day with a cheap wine hangover.

The apartment was hot, and Ashley wasn't sitting in front of an episode of *Law & Order* as was her routine.

The sliding door to the balcony was open, and I heard the types of sniffs that are brought on by heavy crying. I thought someone had died.

"What's wrong?" I asked while putting my hand on her shoulder. I sat down in the chair beside her and saw the sadness swimming around her pupils.

We had stopped subscribing to the idea that we shared a conscience known as Quim and were even embarrassed that we'd once believed we found god in each other, but we never lost the ability to communicate on a higher level. Before she said a word, I knew it was over.

"You're never going to change," she said. The sleeve of her shirt was damp with tears.

"What do you mean?"

"I want more than this." She opened her mouth, but stopped herself and put her hand on my knee.

"Me too," I said.

She squinted her eyes, unleashing a flood of tears. The tangled damp strands of hair that hung across her face were evidence that this had been going on long before I returned home from pouring pitchers and shooting the shit.

"I'm moving back east."

We had started dating as college kids who thought nothing was wrong with taking acid and night swimming, and then became domestic partners who shared a health care plan. We grew into adulthood together. We knew each other's every story, annoying habit, and quirk. We hadn't gone a day in the previous seven years without talking or texting.

When I found out my dad had to have surgery to remove a potentially cancerous lymph node from his neck, she held me for an hour without saying a word.

When she didn't make the Seattle Seagals after passing the first two auditions, I made her mac and cheese to help her look on the bright side. "At least you can give up your cheerleader diet," I said.

I knew I could always make her laugh when we were leaving the house, and I'd speak in poor Spanish, saying "*Donde esta los sacapuntas,*" when I meant "Where are my keys?"

She knew I hated dancing at weddings and never tried to drag me on the floor for "YMCA." During a slow one she would seductively walk toward me with her hand out, then escort me to the least crowded section of the dance floor and rest her head on my neck. As I tried my best to move my feet in sync with hers, she'd make a smart remark about another guest. "Did you see Pants McGhee?"

We traveled to Europe, Australia, Mexico, and Canada together. I met everyone in her family, and her mom even had a pet name for me, "Stupid Steven." We were in love when we boarded a cross-country flight that had been delayed five hours. We kept our spirits up in the terminal knowing we'd at least get a movie on the plane. When it turned out to be *The Lake House*, she made me cry with laughter as she commented on the absurdity of the plot. "Let me get this straight—Keanu can send magic letters in a mailbox, but can't make magical dinner reservations?"

One time at a party we lost track of each other, and I got caught in a conversation with a drunk guy who was trying to convince me that Dave Matthews was the great musician of our generation.

"I've seen him live fifty-seven times," he said as he held on to the wall for support. "Dude can play guitar."

"He doesn't totally suck," I said.

"Fuck no." He pushed himself off the wall and, as he struggled to stand up straight, fell back against it. "He doesn't suck." He put his beer bottle to his lips and continued speaking, causing him to spray my face with foam when he shouted, "He's the best in the world!"

I was trying to think how to respond when I felt Ashley behind me. She slipped a hand in my front pocket and then bit down on my earlobe. "Meet me at the car in five minutes. I want to fuck."

When we returned to the party and people questioned our silly grins, we told them we went out to smoke a joint—keeping it a secret that we just fogged up the windows of my car for the third time that day.

She was able to excite me in a way I'd never felt with other girls. Our connection was so deep that I didn't feel insecure when telling her that nothing got me hotter than being pulled from a crowded situation for a quickie. My complete trust in her allowed me to be vulnerable enough to expose my desires, resulting in the best sex of my life.

As she wiped her nose on her sleeve, I noticed just how beautiful she was.

"My flight leaves in a week," she said.

"I'm going back to the bar."

Something changed between us during those final four days. The tension was lifted. We actually talked about things other than TV shows and food. We sat on the carpet and divided up our CDs and books.

"You should keep all the Vonnegut," I said. "You're a much bigger fan than I am."

"Thanks. You can keep the Bukowski."

Then, one morning I woke and she was gone. While I worked that day I found myself looking around the apartment and noticed the lack of her presence. The bare spots on the bookshelf, her shoes that used to line the front hallway, and the photos missing from the wall that I told her to keep.

I moved to a cheaper apartment that had drafty windows and a slow-draining shower. I rarely cooked and sometimes went whole weeks where my only human interaction was an email exchange with Phitten about which hotels spelled *hair dryer* as one word and which ones broke it into two.

When I couldn't sleep I listened to Elliot Smith and wrote reflective poetry with bad hourglass metaphors. Had Brian and I still been making chapbooks, I'd have put one together called *Employed Adult. What the Fuck Am I Doing?*

Three months after Ashley left, I turned thirty years old. It didn't feel much different than any other day. I spent my lunch break slurping ramen noodles while scrolling through my Facebook feed, filled with new homes and babies. I was clicking an obligatory "like" on a photo of an old friend's kid when I got a message.

Steve, I just want to say thank you for all your hard work over the past few years. You've been a great help. I wish you the best of luck in all your future endeavors. Feel free to put me down as a reference.

I responded immediately.

I'm not quite sure what this email means? Is there something I should know?

Haven't you spoken with your agency? Friday is the last day of your contract. They should have told you.

It had been a year since I'd spoken with my agency, and I stopped paying attention to my contract expiration dates. I wasn't given benefits and didn't get paid time off like a full-time employee, but four years of service had caused me to stop thinking of myself as a temp. The work never slowed down, so why would they get rid of me?

I put in minimal effort my final two days by spending most of the time browsing job sites and looking into unemployment benefits. When I hit publish on my final hotel description, I closed the laptop and looked around my apartment. The bookshelf displayed the spines of authors I aspired to be like, and the photos on the wall were of people I admired, but had never met. Everything was mine. There was no evidence I'd spent the previous eight years of my life intertwined with a woman I hadn't spoken to in months. Unemployment was something I would have to face alone. I worried how I was going to pay my rent, but was thankful I didn't have a mortgage.

Temporary Madness

In my father's capitalism, employees were nurtured by their company and encouraged to learn new skills. Today's major corporations hire disposable temp workers to do the work of a full-time employee, without the obligation of providing benefits. Temp workers are familiar with dead ends—they are hired with a predetermined exit date. The moment they feel comfortable in a role, the contract expires, and it's on to the next job.

After eight years of this, I badly wanted a change. I tried my hand at freelance writing, but after six months and only $950, I got a call from a job recruiter who told me I'd be "perfect for" a job at Amazon. She had found my LinkedIn profile and, because of my past experience temping twice at Amazon and twice at Expedia, thought I would be an excellent candidate for a job assisting Amazon Fulfillment Centers with mis-ships and lost inventory.

I don't know how I feel about being "perfect" for the job of handling a customer return on a pair of pink Skechers. There was a one-in-a-million chance that my parents would meet and produce me. My time on Earth is precious. Making sure a woman in Topeka, Kansas, has the right pair of sneakers to wear to Zumba class doesn't feel like the zenith of my time here on the planet. If I'm hit by a bus tomorrow, I doubt I will find any comfort knowing I spent valuable time helping people get the right exercise attire delivered to their front door in a timely and inexpensive manner. That said, I was desperate for the money. I accepted the position.

On Monday morning, I rode the elevator up nine stories while fantasizing about a Marxist uprising where temps took control of the means of production and held Jeff Bezos hostage until he conformed to a socialist belief system where temp workers are valued as more than just cogs in his world-dominating machine. When the doors opened I followed a train of other temps—dropping our sandwiches in the fridge, filling our mugs with coffee, then scattering to our desks to hunker down for the next eight hours.

I'm an adequate temp. I work hard enough that the higher-ups leave me alone, but not so hard that I can't find twenty minutes a day to tinker with my fantasy football team. Knowing the job has no future makes it difficult for me to find the motivation to put on my best performance. And yet, somehow, Amazon keeps hiring me.

Amazon temps are brought on for a trial basis that lasts a maximum of eleven months. The temp must sink or swim. Those who tread water have their contract renewed, while those who can't perform are left to drown. I can sympathize when I see a new hire looking lost and confused. The first week of a new contract consists of a brief introduction and a link to outdated SOPs and wikis, leaving the new employee to ask the people around him how to do his job. Once a new employee feels slightly comfortable, management will send an instant message with a list of common mistakes.

Some temps love it when the new hire needs to be trained. They assume the role of lead temp because they take pleasure in the feeling of importance that comes with pointing out someone else's errors. I swear I can see a suppressed grin when a senior temp gets to say "Steven, I need to speak with you."

One guy, who was enjoying his senior status a little too much, used the phrase "I need to see you in my office," which was really his desk littered with half-empty bottles of peach iced tea and crammed into the corner of a room housing ten other temps. "Do you understand this?" he asked me. "I don't want to see you make this mistake again."

I was aware of the mistake but hadn't cared enough to correct it. I had hoped no one would notice, or at least that by the time someone did notice, my contract would have expired and I'd be working my next temporary job.

"I'm going to have to pay more attention to your work," he continued.

I felt sad for him that he cared so much. It was his first contract out of college, and there was hope in his eye. I wanted to grab him by the shoulders and shout, "Don't you realize none of this matters? What do you think we've got left, thirty to forty years? Have you ever had a Washington peach? The season just started! They're so juicy. Way better than that artificial stuff you drink. Let's hitchhike to the country. We can pull peaches right off the branch and eat them watching the sunset. Let's remind ourselves what is real."

Instead I said, "Sure thing, guy."

Some temps bought into his act and behaved as if he was their boss. It created a hierarchy like high school. The most senior temps were in charge and took ownership of the comfortable couch in the casual conference room during meetings. They stopped timing their lunch breaks and dipped out fifteen minutes early whenever management was too occupied crunching the numbers to notice. The temps who'd done six months were the juniors. They were still full of confidence that they'd be that rare person who managed to transform his or her contract into a full-time job. They tried to buddy up with management by finding out what video games they played or the TV shows they watched, and they said things like "Bazinga" when they got coffee next to the manager who wore a *Big Bang Theory* T-shirt under his unzipped hoodie. The sophomores had been on contract for two months and were starting to feel comfortable. A few fell into a routine and knew where to get coffee and what day of the week the grilled cheese food truck showed up. They were still considered newbs by everyone else except the temps who just started.

I never bought into these roles. The hierarchy was meaningless. I just wanted to do my time and get out with as few beatings as possible. From the time I sat down at my desk until the time I left for the day, I wore my headphones. Even if nothing was playing, they acted as earplugs shutting out the office. The unfortunate result was that I spent all my time working. I was resolving more cases than was expected of such a new employee. I didn't even take my government-mandated fifteen-minute breaks—not because I was trying to impress, but because I feared that any time I stood up from my chair I was opening myself up to conversation. I would be happy to make small talk about a recent ballgame, but all they ever wanted to talk about was work.

"Can you believe Apple has stopped calling the black iPod 'black' and replaced it with 'space gray'? We're going to have to make so many changes. You thinking about working this weekend?" My mind would wander whenever I found myself in one of these pointless conversations. I imagined climbing on the top of my desk, breaking my laptop over my knee, throwing the pieces in the air, and then yelling "life is more than a paycheck," but I instead smiled and nodded and waited for the appropriate moment to put my headphones back on.

Unbeknownst to me, my antisocial work method was noticed. I went from freshman to sophomore in two weeks. I was told that I would be shadowed by a new employee. After two weeks of successfully speaking less than fifty words a day, I would have someone next to me for eight hours straight. It was my job to explain each step I took to resolve a case. I liked to jokingly refer to Bezos as the Serpent King, but the fact that I would spend two days in my own personal hell made me consider he might actually have a forked tongue behind his sinister smirk.

I had openly criticized him before. After completing my previous Amazon contract, I published an "Open Letter to Jeff Bezos."

Dear Jeff Bezos,

In your position, I imagine that you rarely have an opportunity to receive feedback from one of your temporary-contract employees. I thought you should have some input. I hope you find this useful.

Having just completed my maximum of eleven months of contract work Amazon allows, I thought I would share my thoughts on your practice of hiring a staff that is made up of temporary-contract workers. Although it may seem like the company is saving money—because you don't have to provide temporary workers with medical coverage or paid vacation time—the revolving door of new hires encourages low quality work, inconsistent productivity, and wastes useful resources on training.

I joined the X-Ray for TV and Movies development team in its infancy. The product hadn't even launched yet. It was exciting to watch the product grow and have input on creating the best possible user experience.

My team leader was an experienced manager, with the ability to adapt to the ever-changing process, and gave the rest of the team confidence that we could go to him with questions or feedback, and he would give it careful consideration. It felt like we were all learning together. Our coding tool was constantly being updated based on worker feedback, and our guidelines were always subject to change. Each new development was covered in our weekly stand-up meeting. If something seemed to get missed or lost in translation, an impromptu meeting was called to get everyone on the same page, which proved to be an effective training method.

One day, that all changed. Our experienced team leader was transferred to a different department. A few of the temps, who had been on the project since X-Ray's inception, applied for the now vacant position of project manager. I was convinced the position would be filled by one of two individuals who had trained me and acted as point people for questions and concerns when the manager was in a meeting. None of the temps who applied for the position got it, which most of us on the team found confusing because they were basically already doing the job.

An outsider was brought in who knew nothing about X-Ray. I was later told the new manger was hired based on management experience. She spent her first week being trained by one of the temps who had been deemed unqualified for the project manager position. After spending a week training the manager, and being her go-to person for the next three weeks whenever there was a problem, he was let go because he reached the maximum of eleven months on his contract. Since the new manager never completely grasped the program, she asked a select few of the oldest temps to train the newest temps. It seemed to me that these people were not chosen based on merit or capability, but more like she was putting together her own collection of "cool" kids. The best way to be put in a leadership role was be a pretty girl or a dude who used liberal amounts of Axe hair gel.

As experienced temps left and new ones rolled in, the breakdown began. Temps who had not paid attention in training were now training new temps. Different temps were teaching different techniques, and it wasn't long before the quality of work suffered. As witness to the poor quality, I made a few attempts to express my concerns, but none of my suggestions were implemented. When one of the higher-ups checked our work and realized that mistakes were being overlooked, performance scorecards were implemented.

The oldest temps would grade the newest temps. If a temp made twenty mistakes in a week, they were let go. I agree that if someone makes that many mistakes they don't deserve the job, but perhaps these mistakes were caused by a lack of proper training. Even though I performed excellent work, I was not deemed worthy of a full-time position, yet I held the fate of someone's job in my hands. We were told the scorecards were an attempt to find out what mistakes were most often being made so they could be addressed. This was confusing since nearly everything I checked had the same mistakes, yet they were never addressed. Of the current X-Ray team, only about half know the guidelines and proper procedure.

By my final month, it was difficult to care. I did quality work. I was one of only a handful of employees who didn't need their work checked before pushing it to live status, but as far as the rest of the team was concerned, I'd lost my enthusiasm for the project.

Why should anyone care if X-Ray succeeds or fails? If X-Ray becomes the biggest program on the planet and puts another several million dollars in your bank account, people in my position will still be sent packing at the end of eleven months. There will always be an endless supply of replacements, and they will be paid less since the pay rate of the team decreased with every new batch of hires. My replacement will probably work really hard for about six months and then realize that they are cruising toward a dead end. They might start caring a little less.

In this terrible economy, I am grateful for the work, and the fact that I have a bachelor's degree and the ability to write a complete sentence means I will probably be back on the Amazon campus in a different department one day. It is likely many of the temps from the X-Ray team will be back as well, but know if they are wearing a green badge, you won't be getting their full potential.

There's a lot of talk about how Amazon is a great place to work. They have showers in the basement. You can get your bike serviced while you work. And there are food trucks!

But if you really want to create a positive work environment and generate productivity and employee loyalty, give your employees some job security.

Amazon is a large company and I know this experience is not unique to me. The company is at a disadvantage when the employees are not working to their full potential.

Sincerely,

Steven Barker

PS: In my final team meeting, we were told that you watched *Dumb & Dumber* using X-Ray. I did the quality assurance on that film. I hope you appreciate my credit timing for Cam Neely in the bathroom scene. We spent an afternoon discussing that one.

The letter gained so much attention that Amazon had to release an official response: "no comment." I figured that riff had destroyed any chance of being rehired, but the background check they performed on me must not have included a Google search, at least not one that went past the fifth page (the first five pages are dominated by Steven Barker the child murderer). It's not until page six that you get to Steven Barker the disgruntled Amazon employee. For a brief moment I did consider maybe this had been part of Bezos's plan to get even with me. Bezos, Beelzebub, they're not far off.

My trainee turned out to be a decent guy, apart from a mild case of halitosis, and even though I was uncomfortable with the situation, I explained to him what I was doing as he looked on and took notes.

Occasionally he stopped me and asked, "Why did you do that?"

My most common response was "because that's what they told me to do." I think one of the reasons I have succeeded in the temp world, if there is such a thing as "success" in the temp world, is that I never look for logic. I simply do what is asked of me. I play the part of the tool they want me to be and let them use me up until it's time to put me back in the drawer.

There were times when I knew I wasn't teaching him correct procedure because I had forgotten the correct way and had figured out a way to solve the issue on my own that didn't result in a lecture from management. As far as I was concerned, that was just as good.

When training was complete, the new guy was sent out on his own. I had helped him out as best as I could and watched him get better, and it wasn't long before we were on the same playing field. Later, he would train someone the incorrect procedures I taught him and maybe add a few incorrect procedures of his own. Meanwhile, Amazon would continue to gain more control over every aspect of the consumer's life while rotating in new temps every eleven months. Whether Amazon chooses to invest in its employees or not, it won't be long before Amazon has a hand in every purchase made on Earth. But helping Bezos achieve that goal is meaningless to me, because I'd rather spend my time seeking out trees that produce delicious peaches.

If I had to place myself in the temp hierarchy, I'm that guy who's too old to be hanging out at high school, but has nothing better going on. I want to leave the windowless rooms and strive for greatness, but I'm complacent. I'm not much different than the drones Bezos plans to use to deliver Skechers to Topeka, Kansas.

Saved by the Unemployment

The uncertainty that comes with unemployment can easily make for an existence that revolves around Netflix binges and afternoon couch naps, a routine I'd fallen into before and then regretted when I finally landed a new contract. I told myself that during my next stint of unemployment I would be more productive.

I kept my promise, and two months after my latest contract expired I was dropping a period at the end of a seventy-five-thousand-word novel I'd tangled into a confusing knot.

Why I chose to make the narrator a married dentist with a daughter still baffles me. I was a temp, with commitment issues and no experience caring for a child. I didn't even have dental insurance. I wasted an afternoon researching the name of that silver-scraper-thing used to clear the plaque between teeth, only to be disappointed when I learned it was called a dental probe and not something more medical sounding.

I saved the two-hundred-page document and hid it in a folder called Works in Progress. I needed it off my desktop because I couldn't bear to watch it die, in the same way a killer covers his victim's eyes to avoid seeing them suffer. I mourned by going for a six-mile run.

After a shower and half a box of mac and cheese, I was still bereaved about the death of my book and not ready to start writing something new. My unemployment benefits weren't enough to cover luxury expenses, like seeing a movie or having a pint at the bar. All I could think to do was turn on the TV. I wanted the day to pass so I could wake the following morning and start a new project, which featured a character living a life I understood—although not something as cliché as an unemployed, failed novelist.

I watched a string of commercials for trade schools, online GED programs, and malpractice lawyers, until coming across a few familiar faces.

Like the majority of my generation, I watched *Saved by the Bell* most days after school. I can still quote some of the more memorable lines. "I'm so excited, I'm so . . . I'm so scared," Jessie said in a very special episode about the dangers of caffeine-pill abuse. I credit that episode as the reason I've never experimented with over-the-counter uppers. Seeing that there was an eight-episode marathon, I put on my no-chance-of-leaving-the-apartment sweatpants and prepared to return to Bayside High after a ten-year absence.

I could understand the conflicts presented in each episode. I related to the insecurity Kelly felt when she got a zit two days before prom. When Lisa's careless spending put her in credit card debt, I knew exactly what it felt like to suffer from financial anxiety. I didn't relate to the comfort in knowing that after the final commercial break all problems would be solved and everything would return to normal. I didn't even know what my normal looked like—was I unemployed or employed? I regularly switched between both, yet neither felt normal. At least any time a situation was approaching normal, it changed, whether it was a job ending or a job beginning. I regularly had to adapt to a new routine.

I had spent every day for two months working on a novel, because I made a commitment to spend unemployment focused on writing.

Unfortunately, it wasn't good writing. My main character was so flat he'd fit into an episode of *Saved by the Bell*. He could be the dentist in an episode where Kelly loses a tooth after accidentally biting down on a promise ring Zack hid in a slice of cake. But it didn't matter that the book would never be read by anyone other than me. Every writer has to complete a bad novel before they can create anything worthwhile. Unemployment granted me that gift. The next morning I opened a new Word document and didn't turn on the TV for a week.

PART II

11:00 a.m.

Hunger hits at 11:00 a.m., but it's too early for a break. You hold out as long as possible because you know when your turkey sandwich is gone, the only thing you'll have left to look forward to is the bus ride home.

Having the freedom to decide when to take lunch is the only thing you like about the job. The second half of the day always moves slower. The later you break, the less time on the clock when you return.

Today is especially slow because you've been working in XML and find yourself checking your personal email every time you complete a new schema of code. You can't help but get distracted. If you didn't escape the matrix every once in a while, you'd go cross-eyed from staring at endless lines of brackets and slashes.

You feel a quick endorphin drip when you see a "(1)" appear on the Gmail tab at the bottom of the screen. You open the page, and the jolt of pleasure you just got evaporates when you read the subject line—"New features, more control: updated Mobile Banking app." You delete the message without opening it.

Days are slower when you don't have someone on the outside who cares how the day is going and wants to arrange dinner plans. There was a time when your inbox was fertile and every email generated an immediate response, but that changed after the breakup. You haven't fully adapted to single life and have moments when you come across an article you know she would like and think to send her a link, only to stop yourself when you remember she's gone.

You've been working this contract for six months and have yet to eat in the break room. Even when you worked a Saturday, and there were only ten people on the floor, there was still too much risk you'd be forced into small talk during your only moment of contentedness of the day. It's not that your coworkers are bad people; it's just that the work drains your ability to be social.

You like the winter because it increases the possibility that the park bench that faces away from your office will be vacant. It's your favorite. When it's occupied, you walk the block while eating your sandwich, which is just as enjoyable. Your only real goal for lunch is solitude. It's the reason you've brought a turkey sandwich to work every single day for as long as you can remember. Anything that requires heating up or a utensil would force you into the break room.

You hit play on a podcast and take satisfying bites as you stare across the park. The sandwich tastes especially good because it has lettuce. You'd like to have lettuce every day, but as a bachelor it's difficult to justify buying a whole head, unless you have plans for using it as more than just a sandwich enhancer.

Last night you had a salad with your frozen pizza and you're determined to keep up that routine. You like the sense of victory that comes with consuming a whole head of lettuce before it goes bad. It's a feeling of accomplishment you never get after completing a project at work.

You finish eating, but aren't ready to go back. You're waiting for the end of a *Moth* story about parents. Usually, you finish listening on the trip back to your desk, but hearing Tig Notaro talk about the sudden death of her mother has you close to tears. You're worried what your coworkers might think if they find you sobbing in the elevator.

It's strange what makes you cry these days. You didn't cry after the breakup, but two days later you wept uncontrollably at the end of *School of Rock*, when the shy girl takes the stage and shows off her amazing singing skills. If you weren't returning to the office you would have shed a tear with Tig.

You notice the break room is empty and pour a green tea. The people you pass on the way to your desk aren't interested in sharing more than a head nod of acknowledgement. You place the tea in the ring stain where your coffee usually sits and check your personal email. One message with the subject line "Ready to buy a home?" You hit delete.

A Hippie, a Punk, and a Privileged Boy

Dallas

My fingers reeked like Long John Silver's taint, even though I'd spent an hour scrubbing them under a burning hot faucet.

"Told you it sucks," Andy said, sitting on the trunk of his car, parked behind a gas station. Earlier that day I'd worked my first shift at the Fish Market. Like a bunch of my friends, Andy had also worked there a few months before quitting. The shop was notorious for a revolving staff of stoners and dropouts. The work was hard and the money sucked, but it paid under the table, which is why it was attractive to kids who hung out in the back of a gas station—the type of kids who couldn't work at Subway because of an arrest record.

I couldn't get a job as a sandwich artist either, but not because of an arrest—those documents were sealed. I didn't have a green card. My dad's work visa hadn't yet extended to the rest of the family and the ten bucks a week allowance he gave me for mowing the lawn and shoveling the driveway wasn't enough to support my suburban teenage lifestyle. The money would be in my pocket on Monday then spent at the record store on Tuesday.

When I was fourteen, I went to the fish market with a friend to pick up dinner and the guy behind the counter noticed the shiny gold hoop dangling from my ear. "What are you, some kind of faggot?" he said.

I was so shocked I didn't know how to respond and nervously smiled.

"If my son came home with one of those I'd rip it out of his head."

Had it not been for that experience, I would have applied for a job their much earlier, but I couldn't imagine working with someone who acted that way toward a customer.

I gave in when my parents announced they were leaving my brother, sister, and me alone for a week and I wanted extra money for party favors.

It only took a quick phone call to land the job. Employee turnaround was so frequent they offered the position to anyone who expressed interest. I showed up on my first day with matching gauged earrings. I convinced myself I was making a statement by leaving them in, but actually I couldn't get them out. They'd been sealed shut with pliers.

The guy who two years prior had offered unsolicited advice on my decision to accessorize unsurprisingly didn't work there anymore, and his replacement, a pale-faced eighteen-year-old named Dallas, didn't care that I had earrings. By then it was 1996 and times had changed. Harrison Ford rocked a diamond on one lobe. Dallas found other ways to humiliate me.

"Don't cut yourself, because we'll have to throw away the fish if there's blood on it," he said as I gutted sea bass for the first time in my life.

It was hard to know what repulsed me more, handling fish guts or the way Dallas acted. He blasted Dave Matthews in the morning and spent forty-five minutes every afternoon in the bathroom with a stack of porno mags. His girlfriend favored midriff-exposing tie-dye T-shirts that displayed her beat-up belly button ring. She hung out behind the counter during his shifts. If she felt like I wasn't working hard enough she would tell me to take out the trash or sweep the front walkway.

One time I gave a customer change for a twenty when she paid with a ten. She was polite enough to point out the mistake, and told me she had done the same thing when she was a cashier at Dairy Queen.

"Dumbass," Dallas's girl said under her breath as I thanked the woman for her honesty.

Two days later I was preparing salads to be sold in a glass case in the front of the store. I was tossing the brown lettuce when Dallas grabbed my arm. "We don't waste." He pulled a handful of lettuce from the trash and sprinkled it over the caesar I was in the middle of constructing. "Then just put green lettuce over top."

At the end of the second week my parents left town. My brother and I told my little sister she could have all the ice cream she wanted and play video games in our parents' bed as long as she stayed out of the backyard, where we got drunk with our friends. I donated twenty dollars from my thirty-dollar paycheck to the keg fund.

I tried my best to hang with my brother and his college friends, but passed out in a lawn chair after puking Ice House into a rosebush. I showed up to work two hours late with a pickled brain that pulsated every time Dallas told me to grab something from the basement. He was pissed because he had to unload the morning delivery on his own. I almost threw up when I had to fillet four-day-old tilapia that was going to be used for seafood ravioli. Luckily, there was nothing in my stomach to puke up, as I'd left it all in my mother's garden the night before.

I just wanted to go home and lie down. My mouth tasted like the previous night's beer mixed with acid from all the gags I'd repressed while stuffing ravioli pockets with expired fish. I managed to make it through the day and I was about to clock out when Dallas's girlfriend called me.

"There's still fish guts in the sink. Dallas's not cleaning that shit," she said.

I acted like I didn't hear her and continued out the door.

"Hey!"

I kept going.

When I got home and poured myself a beer from the keg, I realized that ten bucks a week wasn't so bad. I called Dallas and told him I quit.

"Who's going to help me unload tomorrow's delivery?"

"Ask your girlfriend."

"Asshole," he said, then hung up the phone.

Fat Ramones

Fat Ramones was a twenty-one-year-old fat guy with a Ramones tattoo. We worked together in a high-end wine and spirits shop that carried bottles that cost more than either of us made in a month. His paycheck was much bigger than mine because I only worked part-time after high school, while he was there all day, every day, except Sunday because of Connecticut's blue laws.

I'd come across a lot of filthy talkers on the job, but he was the filthiest.

"She could use my tongue as a tampon," he said about a bleached-blonde mother in a sundress picking up a case of Dom Perignon for her son's graduation party. When Fat Ramones wasn't describing immoral acts he fantasized about performing on the various women who patronized the store, he talked about music. "There hasn't been a good punk record since 1983," he said to me on my first day, as he gave me a tour of the basement where we'd spend most of our time.

Our job was to stock shelves, and first thing every afternoon we put away the daily delivery. We took our time carrying boxes of booze down a rickety staircase since we knew that if we finished stocking too quickly we would be assigned boring tasks like dusting bottles or sweeping the back alley. As long as we were in the basement, the owner, Mike, assumed we were working, but most of the time we were listening to a Dead Kennedys cassette and passing the time with stupid games.

"I'm going with Popov today," Fat Ramones said as he pulled a plastic bottle of vodka from an opened case. He took a practice swing in the batter's box we'd outlined on the floor with a red Sharpie.

I grabbed the plastic lime we kept hidden above an air duct and adjusted my crotch. I pretended to spit, then flung the lime between an alley stacked inches from the ceiling with chardonnay and merlot.

The lime connected with the sweet spot of the bottle, sending it blasting back toward my face. I ducked, and it slammed into a case of Moët Brut.

"What the fuck is going on down there?" Mike yelled from the top of the stairs.

"Just putting stuff away," Fat Ramones said as he stuffed the dented bottle behind a shelf.

"I don't want to see the whites of your eyes until everything is put away."

"What an asshole," Fat Ramones said under his breath. "I deserve a flask of Beam for that remark."

I never stole anything because I was a product of Catholic school and afraid of burning in hell. But, more than that, because Mike was way scarier than a pit of eternal fire.

One afternoon, I had run out of things to do and was sitting on the floor of the South American section dusting bottles on the bottom shelf. They didn't need dusting, but it made me look busy enough that Mike left me alone. A woman in a tennis skirt was shopping for a dinner party and had compiled an impressive collection of wines from around the globe at the checkout counter. When she turned down my aisle to browse a row of Chilean *carmenères*, I looked up and caught an accidental peek at her pink panties. I was pretty sure she didn't notice, but I got up so she wouldn't feel uncomfortable. I stood behind the register and thought I was being helpful by boxing up the bottles she had placed on the counter.

"What the fuck are you doing?" Mike whispered in my ear.

I was startled, and I almost dropped a sixty-five-dollar bottle of pinot noir.

"Who told you to box that up?" He put both hands on my shoulders and turned me away from the counter, then pushed.

When she was ready to check out, Mike helped her whittle the fifteen bottles she put on the counter down to twelve that he promised would "delight experienced wine drinkers." I carried the case to her car and she tipped me two dollars.

"Hey, idiot," Mike said when I returned.

"Me?"

"Never box up a customer's order before they've decided what they want."

"My mistake."

"Can you try not to be such a moron?"

"Sorry. It won't happen again."

I retreated out back to give him some time to cool off.

Fat Ramones was sitting on an overturned milk crate sucking a cigarette down to the filter. "Your eyes are red," he said.

"Allergies."

He pulled his pack of 100s from his pocket and lit a fresh one.

"Wanna duck hunt?"

"Sure."

He flicked the cigarette butt in the air, and I watched it spin as I gathered a loogie in the back of my throat. The butt reached its apex, and I fired a glob of spit, catching it in a comet of saliva. The weight of the phlegm forced the butt to the ground, where it splattered on the concrete.

"Nice one," he said.

"Thanks."

Three years later I was back in town for spring break. I was getting a cup of coffee at Dunkin Donuts when I saw Fat Ramones wheeling a hand truck stacked with champagne to a luxury model SUV.

"Hey," I said once he was finished loading the case.

"Hey, man," he said. He lit a cigarette. "Bitch didn't even tip me, but I'd still let her piss on my face."

"How are things?"

"My band might get a gig at the VFW Hall next month."

"Cool," I said.

"You should come."

"I'm just in town for the night. I've got to get back to school."

"I bet that college pussy is ripe, huh?"

"I do okay."

He flicked his cigarette in the air and followed it with his eyes. "Get it," he said. The butt dropped to the ground and rolled into a sewer grate. "Weak."

"Whoops," I said. "I forgot about that."

"Whatever. I gotta go," he said. "You know Mike. If I'm out here too long he'll sodomize me with a bottle of port."

"Sounds about right," I said.

"Fuck that guy." He held out his hand, and I slapped it.

"Good seeing you, man."

"Later." He walked back to the shop dragging the hand truck behind him. The wheels bounced off the ground every time it skipped over a crack the sidewalk.

My Father's Quiz

I was single and unemployed and used the time to write a short story about a couple that had grown apart. I called it fiction, but it was based in reality. When it was complete I didn't submit it to any journals because I realized I'd written it for closure. I tucked it away in a folder, which gave me some relief from the post-breakup depression, allowing me to focus on finding a job.

I created a profile on a job site for freelance writers, and as I considered what type of headshot to use (professional with a tie? but it was freelance work, I thought, so I wondered if pajamas would be more appropriate), I realized that I should be doing the same thing for dating. I didn't mind being single when I had a job, but being single and unemployed was dismal. I went to happy hour with friends, but on rainy nights when nothing was going on and couples stayed in with pizza and a movie, I was drinking beer alone. I needed to find a job or meet someone before the solitude paved a path to depression.

My job profile and dating profile weren't all that different; they both boasted all my best qualities in the hopes of attracting an inquiry. I split my time applying for jobs and dates and woke every morning to double the disappointment when there were no new messages in my inbox. Jobs weren't responding to my writing samples and the women who responded to my date requests always went dark after the third exchange when I revealed I was unemployed.

Online dating was a futile endeavor for the unemployed, but I thought it beneficial to become familiar with the TV show *Freaks and Geeks*, because I saw it listed as a favorite TV show among the girls I was interested in. It would be a useful skill when I was back in action because I'd be able to send opening messages like "Bill is definitely my favorite character, but I was much more like Daniel in high school."

When I finished the series I still wasn't any closer to finding a job. The only new message in my inbox was from my father with the subject line "How's the job search going?" I didn't want to respond until I had something to report. I saved it in a folder containing one other email that had information on a copyediting job that required five to seven years' experience editing at a major newspaper. I held on to that one in case there was a week where I hadn't met my job contact quota and needed something to include in my weekly status report. Even if I exaggerated the work I'd done editing submissions for a small literary journal, I could only fake two years' worth of professional editing experience. There was no chance my resume would make it past the first screener. It was for emergency purposes only, but I'd never come close to needing it. I was averaging two applications a day, which put me way over the government requirement of three a week to retain my unemployment benefits.

I refreshed Craiglist's employment section for the third time in ten minutes, and a blue link appeared atop a stack of grayed-out job postings. "Paid Internship For Writers With The Possibility Of Full-Time Employment!!" It was intriguing enough that I sent off my resume, cover letter, and writing samples. I got an immediate response.

Dear Steven,

Congratulations! You have been selected for the Collective Clicks Paid Writing Internship. You were chosen from amongst a large pool of candidates primarily because we loved your style of writing when you explained why you think you deserve to be accepted as an intern. In the past, writing interns have ended up being employed by Collective Clicks post-internship—so yes, there is a chance for employment after the internship; although obviously no guarantee!

The internship came with a free online writing course that was valued at $150 and, upon completion, a certificate stating that I was an expert review writer. Adding that I was certified in something seemed a valuable addition to my writer profile.

A guy named Izzy monitored my progress and was available for questions. I learned about search engine optimization and how to draw attention to things posted online using keywords and phrases. The course focused on WordPress, which I'd already been using for a year, having mastered the basics after watching a YouTube tutorial, but I still took diligent notes throughout each lesson. I prided myself on getting good grades on the proficiency quizzes, and I completed the course with a final score of forty-nine out of fifty. I was tempted to print it out and hang the results on my refrigerator.

The next step was to use what I had learned and write four product reviews. Though he said it wasn't necessary, Izzy encouraged me to choose products that I used or owned. It was odd that having used the product was not required, but freelance writing often involves writing about subjects I know little about; however, I figured it would be easiest to review familiar products.

It took some digging, but I was able to find four relatively new items to review: an MP3 player, a podcast microphone, a pair of running shoes, and a pair of casual shoes. I analyzed each product and documented the pros and cons. The MP3 player was half the price of an iPod, and half the quality. Even at full blast the music was drowned out by passing trucks when I ran next to the highway. Was it worth the cost? Since it's rare for me to purchase anything over fifty dollars without consulting a review, I felt a responsibility to accurately portray my overall satisfaction with the item. Since an iPod was out of my price range, I was happy with the MP3 player, but advised anyone with the financial capability to get an iPod instead.

I incorporated what I learned in the course when I described my Asics running shoes as "reliable" and "perfect for the weekend trail runner." I included the product name twice in the meta description and included five focus keywords. I sent each completed review to Izzy, who graded them individually out of fifteen points for a total of sixty.

I scored a fifty-eight. I was marked down one point because I'd forgotten to include an image with my running shoe review, and in my microphone review I forgot the product number in the meta description. Izzy said those were minor mistakes, and I was eligible for the paid internship.

To complete the internship I was required to write fifteen reviews that paid two dollars each, which was only paid out if all reviews met Collective Clicks standards.

Izzy sent me a spreadsheet of products that needed reviews and suggested I check Amazon descriptions for items I wasn't familiar with.

My first review was for a men's reserve chronograph blue dial stainless steel watch. I didn't know anything about watches. I found them uncomfortable and had learned early in life that there were enough clocks in the world that I could get by without one. Even in the nineties when rude boy fashion provoked me to get a pocket watch, I stopped wearing it because it hindered my skateboarding.

The watch I had to review retailed at $1,500. In four hundred words I had to describe its look as well as the pros and cons. I found it unlikely that the type of person who'd spend $1,500 on a luxury item would seek out random internet advice, so I wasn't too concerned that my fabricated review would cause someone to make a purchase they'd later regret.

I typed the name of the watch into Google and received five thousand results. I read a description on Amazon and barely understood the terminology. Flame fusion, unidirectional stainless-steel bazel, Swiss Quartz—the terms were foreign to me. Thankfully, my English degree had provided me with excellent bullshitting skills. I used the same technique to write the review as I had when I wrote a paper on a subject I knew little about. I researched and rewrote descriptions I found online in my own words. "Blue dial has matching luminous silver tones" became "the luminous silver tones match the sapphire dial."

It took me an hour to put down four hundred words and I took comfort in the fact that my bullshitting abilities hadn't been diluted since graduation. I impressed myself with lines like "The Swiss-made watches are exclusively handmade and represent a pinnacle in superiority for the discerning aficionado."

The following morning there was an email from Izzy.

Steven,

Great work! Your review will be posted later today with your name in the byline! It's going to look great in your portfolio. I've highlighted your next assignment.

Izzy

My next task was to review a pink Gucci watch strap, designed for women with petite wrists. I thought I knew nothing about watches, but I really knew nothing about Gucci watch straps designed for women with petite wrists. At least a watch had a face with knobs and hands I could describe to fill up the word count, but four hundred words on a piece of leather seemed impossible.

I entered the name into Google and surfed through the top results. All the links led to bargain sites that listed two or three features with no descriptive text. I turned what little info I found about double-stitched leather and solid gold hardware into sentences and managed a modest two hundred words. I gave it a second pass and stretched each sentence. "Secure fold over safety clasp" became "The safety clasp securely folds over your petite wrist." I pulled each sentence apart just far enough that it didn't break and managed to hit the word count.

The next day I had to review a stainless steel watch strap for men, which meant I wouldn't be able to reuse any of the descriptive language I had come up with the previous day. I doubted that even guys with the most delicate wrists would buy something described as "dainty," and the only antonym for dainty I found was inelegant. I was certain no man in the world had ever done an internet search for "inelegant watch strap."

I questioned whether any of this experience would enhance my freelance writer profile. I already had a decent collection of samples showcasing what I could do and I didn't want to bring down the quality by adding a bunch of wordy watch reviews—just like my dating profile wouldn't include a double-chinned selfie in a collection of thought-fully curated photos taken from my most attractive angles. The point of the profile was to only present the best.

My dad taught me to ask myself two questions when faced with uncertainty about a job—does it make me happy and/ or does it make me money? Before I could answer I needed more information.

Izzy,
I have a few questions about the internship. How many people are usually hired on for full-time positions after

the internship is complete? Is the full-time position forty hours a week? What's the average pay? What percent of people complete the internship?

Thanks,
Steven

While waiting for a response, I Googled Izzy and discovered he lived in Florida. I recalled the Criagslist ad stated there was an office in Seattle where the potential full-time job was located. I searched for the posting to make sure I hadn't misunderstood the details, but it had been removed. This sparked my suspicion, which then increased when I stopped and thought about the credibility of someone named Izzy. As far as I was concerned, the name Izzy was only appropriate for guys who played rhythm guitar and had a permanent burning cigarette wedged between the E string and the neck. Not someone responsible for my employment.

Hi Steven,
We usually ask most interns to stay on as freelance writers for us, on an as neede [sic] basis. We pay freelance writers per piece, depending on thier [sic] level of expertise. Price per piece starts at $4.
    Please let me know if you have any additional questions/ concerns.

Izzy

It didn't make me too confident to see that the guy who'd been judging my writing made two obvious typos in his email.

Izzy,
Does that mean there is no opportunity for full-time employment?

Steven,
There is no full-time employment, as in 9 to 5, rather we work with our writers on a freelance basis.

Thanks,
Izzy

Izzy,
Is the only possible work after the internship to write four-hundred-word reviews at two dollars a pop?
I'm sorry if it sounds like I'm being difficult. I'm just trying to figure out what the incentive is to complete the internship and work with you guys.

Steven,
The incentive is that it's excellent work experience—you have a chance to learn specific skills (through the workshops) and then apply them in a real life setting and receive feedback. The feedback we receive from interns who have gone all the way to the end has only been positive.

Here is some real feedback from real people:

- Thank you so much for everything! I learned a lot during my time writing with Collective Clicks and truly enjoyed the experience. I appreciate all you did, thanks!
- Thank you so much for all your guidance . . . have truly enjoyed working with you!
- Thank you so much for this opportunity . . . I really got a lot out of it, and had a great time, too. :)

This is obviously besides for [*sic*] getting the certification. I hope that clears things up for you.

Thanks,
Izzy

I now had enough information to take my father's quiz. Would this work make me happy? No, it would actually make me unhappy. The time spent writing reviews would take away time from doing the writing I was passionate about. Would it make me money? No. It would potentially cost me money. Spending two hours working on a review that paid two dollars was time that could be better spent looking for a real job. Also, I did some research and couldn't find any evidence that the certificate they were offering held any merit in the business-writing world.

Izzy,

Thanks for the opportunity, but I'm not going to learn anything new from writing twelve more reviews on watches
I've never seen. I was "accepted" to this internship from
"a large pool of people" based on my writing samples, so
clearly I don't need to add fifteen watch reviews to it. This
feels to me like a way to exploit new/young writers for
cheap labor. Your ad has been removed from Craigslist,
but I recall there was mention of a Pioneer Square office,
which I can't find any evidence of. Also, your certificate
holds no accreditations in the writing world so that "certificate" means nothing. I guess it's my own fault for trust-
ing someone named Izzy. Just curious, any chance you rip
on rhythm guitar?

Izzy never responded to my email, and I didn't receive
the twelve dollars I earned for the six reviews I'd completed
or a certificate stating I was an expert review writer. Instead
I was self-certified in identifying internet labor scams, a
skill I didn't feel was relevant to my freelance writer profile,
but I did add "detecting internet scams" in the section of
things I was good at in my dating profile.

Had I not been so desperate for contact, I'm sure I
would have been more cautious and caught on to the ruse
after receiving the initial email. The impersonality of it was
an obvious cut-and-paste job I should have recognized.

At least I'd caught on before wasting any more time on
completing the whole course and could focus on important things, like watching *Amelie*, which just like *Freaks*

and Geeks was a favorite movie of all the girls I dug on the dating site. My only concern was that I might have possibly convinced a discerning aficionado to buy an inelegant watch.

In a Room with a Radio

I got drunk the night before my final interview in an effort to present myself as an undesirable employee. I had advanced through multiple stages of the hiring process while hoping that I would eventually receive an email thanking me for my time, but stating I wasn't the right person for the job.

I'd applied during one of my job site rampages, when I'd sent my generic cover letter and resume to every new posting on Indeed.com. I was so determined to fulfill my government-mandated job search requirements that I barely looked at the job descriptions and hadn't realized I applied to a position at Expedia, a company I previously gave four years of my life only to be let go with two days' notice.

I believed administering twenty-dollar hand jobs under a highway overpass more reputable work than returning to a company that offered no loyalty, but six months on the dole made it difficult to rationalize taking a dive. I boasted about my skills and provided examples of how I contributed at my previous jobs.

"Heck yeah, I know SharePoint," I said. "At my last job people came to me with all their SharePoint problems. The office prankster even put a 'SharePoint King' sign on my cubicle one day when I left early for a dentist appointment."

"You sound exactly like the type of person we're looking for," said the gatekeeper at the end of the hiring labyrinth.

I was offered a short-term contract writing promotional copy for cruise liners and, unlike my previous stint at Expedia, this position was on-site. I turned it down. The lack of job security was enough to convince myself I'd made the right choice. It would only be a matter of time before the gig expired and I returned to the exact same situation. However, I was unaware that my unemployment benefits would halt after answering "yes" on my weekly questionnaire when asked, "Did you refuse any work this week?" It was possible I would have known that had I actually read the unemployment packet I was issued instead of using it as a placemat when eating everything bagels in front of the TV. I was also billed $1,400 in back pay since it took three weeks after I clicked "yes" for my checks to be discontinued.

I had money in my savings account and didn't have any debt, so losing my benefits wasn't going to put me on the street. I was confident my bachelor's degree was enough to land me an entry-level office job, or I could always go back to delivering pizza. If things really went south, I could get a loan from my folks.

An on-site role at Expedia paid the same as when I worked from home but required an hour commute across a congested toll bridge. As a temp I didn't qualify for benefits or holiday pay, but at least during my previous stint, I enjoyed the luxury of working from home. The comfort of attending conference calls in my underwear and never having to eat a PB&J in a break room made it easy to over-look the mistreatment and stagnation.

I considered what my life would have been had I accepted the job.

Alarm at 5:00 a.m., in the car by 7:05, I'd choke down cigarettes to keep calm as I fought my way through con-gested lane changes. I'd spend the morning writing consumer-catching words like *luxurious*, *affordable*, and *spacious*. I'd eat lunch alone on a bench outside, even if it was cold, or in my car if it was raining, all the while dreading the moment when I would have to return to my desk. I'd spend the afternoon fighting off a yawn and scroll-ing through Reddit and panicking every time my email chimed, fearing I'd published another typo. I'd smoke two more cigarettes on the ride home, the whole time praying for available parking near my apartment. If I was lucky enough to locate a spot in under fifteen minutes, I'd run to the grocery store; otherwise, I'd be so defeated from cir-cling the block I'd only have enough energy to flip channels until bed. I'd put off doing laundry until the boxer briefs with the broken elastic were the only pair left in the drawer, and I'd spend Saturday drunk and waste Sunday with a hangover.

A few months of near poverty on a diet of Rainier beer and generic brand macaroni and cheese sounded like heaven compared to that life.

The desperation set in when my savings could only sup-port one more month of expenses. Fearing the possibility that I'd have to cash in a CD, which I anticipated growing for at least another ten years, I applied to a Craigslist ad looking for a sexy housecleaner. Half a bottle of Canadian whiskey deep, I took a bathroom mirror selfie while wearing little more than purple rubber gloves. I held a scrubbing brush in front of my face, making sure, if the image ever ended up on /r/gonewild, I'd be unrecognizable.

I never got a response and, honestly, was a little hurt. My abs looked *tight!* Thankfully, one afternoon when I was considering selling off some books and records for gas money, a recruiter offered me a two-week position in a warehouse that manufactured sporting goods.

The pay was significantly lower than what I was used to, but I liked sports and I worked in warehouses throughout college. Unlike office work, warehouse duties had clearly defined goals. The job was done when the truck was loaded or the racks were empty. A completed piece of copy could go through ten drafts before someone decided it was headed in the wrong direction.

"Do you think you could give this another shot?" one of my previous bosses used to say when she was unhappy with my work. "I don't think this is the right message. How about just starting over with fresh new ideas? Really entice the reader! There's a free buffet. It almost writes itself."

Warehouse managers were direct and stated what their expectations were for each project. The work was logical, and the most efficient way of doing something was the only way. Office managers weren't as direct and often used passive-aggression as a means to control your work. After a six-year hiatus, I was kind of looking forward to blue-collar work.

Anticipating that it would be difficult to park, I showed up twenty minutes early. There were vacancies in the warehouse lot, but it was off-limits to temps. When my start time was just a few minutes away, I pulled into a pay lot. The fee was equivalent to one hour of work I hadn't even done yet. I subtracted a few dollars from the budget I already formulated in my head and rushed inside.

"Good," said the baby-faced manager as he evaluated his newest piece of livestock. "You look like you can carry a few boxes."

"I can."

He handed me a cardboard box filled with tags. "These are your sizes. S means small, M means medium, L is—" He stopped himself. "You get it. You're not an idiot. Apply one sticker to each card. When you run out, let me know. There's plenty more."

I hoped that wasn't my only task for the next two weeks. I had been so thankful to get a job I'd forgotten warehouse work could be painfully repetitive.

The rest of the temps each held a box similar to mine, and we traded nervous smiles. We all knew it was best to assess the situation before getting too comfortable. Managers all had their own way of interacting with short-term contractors. Some were grateful to be helped out of a jam and sprang for sandwiches at lunch, while others were against on-the-clock bathroom breaks.

"Really appreciate you all being here," said the project manager. "I'm going to be running around all day, but don't hesitate to stop me if you have any questions. Let's get to work."

There was a beat-up boom box in the corner of the room. The volume knob was missing and the tip of the antenna was kinked. "Kokomo" buzzed out the blown-out speakers and I thought, *with all the great Beach Boys, songs how come that abomination gets the most airplay?*

I considered sharing this contemplation with the group, but figured I should first locate the temp who would be most appreciative of my insight into contemporary pop music. Only then could I present my argument on why "Kokomo" is, without question, the worst Beach Boys song ever recorded. My supporting facts included the detail that Brian Wilson took no part in writing the song, as well as the point that any shred of cool the band still possessed in the early nineties was eviscerated by the music video featuring the cast of *Full House* in neon beach attire.

Across from me sat a woman in her early forties, and based on the way she didn't concern herself with placing the sticker directly in the designated outline, I sensed she'd expected more at this point in her life. Her yogi body and turquoise necklace inspired me to call her Hippie Chick.

At another table sat a dumpy little fella who was blabbing on about a recent trip to Japan to an uninterested frat boy. Dumpy was quite pleased with himself as he regaled Frat Boy with stories about eating eel and seeing cherry blossoms. I would have rather listened to "Kokomo" on repeat than hear about how "they don't even know what a Seattle roll is over there."

"How about you? Are you a traveler like me?" Dumpy asked Frat Boy.

"Not yet. I'd been counting on baseball to provide travel opportunities, but I blew out my shoulder last season."

"The Japanese love baseball."

"Me too," Frat Boy said while placing a hand on his shoulder as he rotated it. "Doc's diagnosis was so bad I lost my scholarship."

"You should study abroad. Japan changed my life."

The girl behind me piped up and said something in Japanese.

Dumpy quickly responded, and even though I didn't understand the language, I could tell whatever he was saying was annoying.

I called the Japanese-speaking girl ComicConQueen. She wore a Zelda T-shirt and had a Hello Kitty backpack. She was unassuming, but I imagined she was the type to spend late nights constructing ambitious costumes to wear at comic book conventions.

We worked in silence until the project manager returned. "Now for the fun part," he said, with the phony enthusiasm of a youth pastor delivering an anti-masturbation sermon. "Now we get to add these cool new labels to replace the old lame ones!"

I barely recognized the difference, but imagined market research showed that a label with an image of a guy scaling a mountain sold more gloves than one without.

"You guys are doing great so far," he said and pulled a box from the cart. "Super awesome, really." He tilted his head forward and put his hand on his chest. "You guys are my homies." He threw a peace sign in the air. "No frontin'."

As I adjusted from sticking stickers on cards to replacing old tags with new ones, I tried to figure out what time it was based on the songs I'd heard.

First was that atrocity "Kokomo," followed by a Phil Collins song I called "Take a Look at Me Now," even though I'm sure that's not the title. Then a Macy's Christmas commercial made me think about a time in kindergarten when a classmate got a nosebleed during the holiday concert. The irony that it happened during "Rudolf the Red Nosed Reindeer" had never occurred to me. Somehow I'd gone my whole life seeing an image of little Scotty Northrep's nose pouring blood every time I thought of Rudolf, without making a red nose connection. I lost track of the next few songs while noodling on that revelation, eventually coming to in the middle of "Love Shack."

"Finally a good one," I said to Hippie Chick.

"Not bad," she responded without looking up.

"'Rock Lobster' is probably my favorite jam of theirs, but this one is good too."

"I don't know that one."

"The bass line might be one of the best in music history," I proclaimed. A fact I only partially believed, but thought might spark a conversation.

It didn't.

Two hours later the project manager returned. "Looks like you guys could use a break," he said. "There's water and coffee down the hall. Sodas on the second floor, but those will cost you a buck and a quarter. Let's meet back here in fifteen minutes."

The room emptied to the first few chords of Springsteen's "Born to Run." I didn't want to miss the best song of the day and found myself staring out the window at a busy street with no crosswalk. A woman in heels waited for the perfect moment to cross four lanes of traffic. She had a bulky purse tucked under one arm and balanced four cups of coffee in the other. She stutter-stepped into the road and then pulled back when a car appeared in the distance. Two more cars passed and she looked down at her watch. She stepped into the first lane, only to retreat when the sound of a motorcycle engine cut through the air. After it sped by, she clumsily stepped into the road. An oncoming pickup truck slowed to a stop as she crossed the four lanes. Her apologetic smile was returned with a middle finger.

That afternoon, I played a game in my head where I tried naming the title and artist of each song before the DJ announced it. I was really good at titles, but had difficulty with the band names. Tuxedo Junction, Nick Gilder, who were these people? When a really good forgotten song came on, I made a mental note to add it to a playlist when I got home.

"They don't make songs like this anymore," I said to Hippie Chick when the Patti Smith Group's "Because the Night" came on.

"I love her," she said while putting down the glove she was working on and looked up at me for the first time all day. "Have you read her memoir?"

"I've been meaning to. I heard it's great."

"If you're a fan, you've got to. It's so good."

Patti was a conversation starter, and we talked about our favorite local running trails and our mutual fondness of western Washington.

"My girlfriend and I spent five years living in a cabin in the woods."

"That sounds peaceful," I said. "I imagine it was a great place to run."

"It was gorgeous, but it's hard to make money out there. Logging is the only industry, and I'm not cut out for that."

"Few people are."

"I worked a few jobs with the parks department," she said.

I looked across the table at her hands as she pressed each sticker into the cardboard. Her thick fingers and tightly trimmed nails gave off the impression she was more comfortable digging in the dirt than working in an office.

"Must have been nice to work outside all day."

"I loved it. It was just too bad their budget couldn't support any new full-time staff members."

"Lame."

When I got back to my apartment later that day, I loaded my iPod with Patti Smith then went for a run. By mile four I'd burned off the nervous energy built up from doing the same motion all day and was content knowing the next two weeks of my life came with a paycheck.

The repetitive nature of the work caused my mind to wander. Hearing New Edition's "Candy Girl" reminded me of

Bobby Brown's "My Prerogative," sparking the memory of a dance routine my friends and I performed at a third grade talent show. I had a mock debate in my head between the principal and a concerned parent after witnessing ten-year-old me simulating sex with a microphone stand.

The radio planted jumping-off topics for me to ponder, like a critique on the fact that, although commercially more successful, and with the exception of "Janie's Got A Gun," everything Aerosmith produced sober was inferior to the songs recorded when Tyler and Perry's drug use was so out of control they were dubbed the Toxic Twins. Or the realization that Journey's "Don't Stop Believing" can make any moment feel significant.

I spent a whole afternoon debating with myself on whether "Roxanne" was an amazing song or one of the worst ever written. I was torn. I always turned it up when it came on in the car, but was it good? It couldn't be. It was pop-reggae sung in falsetto. Nothing about that made sense, just like the lyric "you don't have to put on the red light." How does Sting know she doesn't have to turn on the red light? I bet under different circumstances she'd love not to put on the red light, but she's got bills to pay. If he's telling her she doesn't have to turn on the red light, he needs to offer an alternative. I'd appreciate Sting's suggestion more if he followed, "You don't have to sell your body to the night," with "because I found you a stable nine-to-five that comes with benefits, a dental plan, and a matching 401(k)."

Had I taken the other job and spent the day writing marketing content, my mind would never have had wondered further than my favorite pizza toppings.

The second week we were tasked with rebranding balaclavas. I pretended like I knew what those were, but thought, *is a Greek dessert considered sportswear?* Then I realized a balaclava was what I'd been ignorantly referring to as a bank robber mask.

"Now you get to use these hella neat guns," said the project manager, holding up a pink pistol with a needlepoint barrel. He pointed it at me and turned his wrist. "Break yo self fool."

"Nice," I said then nodded my head to let him know I caught the reference.

"I need you guys to snip off the old labels, then use this gun to attach the new ones," he said while demonstrating the process. "This isn't my regular job, but sometimes I go upstairs and help because it's so much fun."

I snipped the label off the first balaclava, then poked the barrel through the fabric and pulled the trigger. As I got comfortable with the process, I recognized the subtle beginning of "Radar Love." I snipped another, attached another, snipped, attached, snipped, attached. *We've got a thing, and it's called radar love.*

I was about to answer "Golden Earring" in my mental game show when the gun misfired and broke my skin.

I sucked the blood and wiped my fingers across the back of my jeans.

Snip, attach, snip, attach, snip, STAB.

Frat Boy looked up at me with concern, "Did you nick yourself?"

"This song makes me want a fast car," I said as I tried to distract attention from the blood trailing down my hand.

"Yowza," the project manager said when he noticed my flesh wound. "You need medical attention."

"It's nothing," I said.

"Let's get a Band-Aid on that, so we don't ruin the merchandise."

"Sorry," I said.

"Happens all the time. Up on the fifth floor they can't keep Band-Aids in stock."

"There are people who do this every day?"

"How else would we get the tags on the gloves?"

"A machine, maybe," I said then found a new appreciation for tag adders across the globe. "I'm surprised you haven't sought cheaper labor overseas."

Before he had a chance to respond, Frat Boy approached holding up a bloody hand.

"Welcome to the medical tent," the project manager said. He handed Frat Boy a Band-Aid. "I have to go take a call, be careful out there."

"Imagine having to do this every day," Frat Boy said while bandaging himself up.

"That would be awful."

Frat Boy and I spent the afternoon talking about sports. He told me about his injury and how he'd originally planned on entering the minors after college, before getting hurt.

"I guess I'll start focusing on class now," he said.

At the end of the day, we exchanged information and talked about meeting up for a beer.

When I drove home I got stuck in traffic because a Mariners game had just let out. I listened to talk radio in an effort to drown out the car horns.

A story came on NPR about a suicide protest at a Chinese factory. One hundred and fifty workers threatened to leap to their deaths if their working conditions weren't improved. After a two-day standoff they were coaxed down. Suicide was so common at that factory they installed nets to catch jumpers. I'd never worked job conditions so bad that I considered taking my own life, but there were mornings where I prayed to be involved in a minor car accident, just so I'd have an excuse to take the day off.

One day during the second week, Hippie Chick showed up an hour late because she'd had a job interview. She'd been out of work for two years, and this was the furthest she'd gone in the hiring process since being unemployed.

"I don't want to be too confident," she said. "That's bit me in the ass before. Who knows how many other people were also applying?"

"I know the feeling," I said. "I've walked out of at least five interviews over the past few months and thought, *nailed it*, only to never hear from them again."

Later that day, Frat Boy and I returned from lunch at the same time. Since we weren't official employees we didn't have access to the employee elevator and had to use the freight elevator. When we got in, it had already been called so we were brought up to the fifth floor instead of the third. The gate opened to a large room with rows of stations about a foot apart from one another. The room was filled with foreign chatter, and women were hunched over boxes of mittens. Michael Jackson's "Beat It" was playing on the radio, and they were all nodding their heads while pulling gloves from boxes and clipping on the new tags. They worked with such grace and speed that Frat Boy and I just looked at each other, slack-jawed. We didn't say anything, but I'm sure we were both thinking, *they're a lot better at this than we are.* They all had smiles on their faces.

A man pushing a cart stacked high with boxes got in the elevator with us.

"You go down," he said.

"Yeah, we go down," Frat Boy said.

As it got closer to 5:00 p.m., it became clear that we weren't going to finish the remaining thirty boxes before the end of the assignment.

"Hey, dudes," the project manager said. "So, I bet you're all thinking, this job is so much fun, does it have to be over?"

Frat Boy looked over at me and rolled his eyes.

"How would you like to work a few more days?" He picked a needle gun off the table and pointed it at his temple. "Can any of you stay? Please don't make me do it."

"I can," I said.

"Thank you," he said and pulled the gun away from his head. "Anyone else?" He brought the gun back to his head. "Don't make me do it."

"Sure," ComicConQueen said.

"You're a lifesaver," he said.

On Monday morning there was a new temp because the others weren't able to return. Hippie Chick got the job she applied to and Frat Boy went back to school to help out with baseball tryouts, even though he was no longer a player on the team. I didn't know Dumpy's reason, but I was sure it was stupid.

The project manager had to get back to his regular work and asked if ComicConQueen and I would be comfortable training the new guy.

"Absolutely," ComicConQueen said.

She could handle training on her own, so I stepped back and she took the lead.

"You've got to be really careful that you're matching the right label with the right product," she said while opening a fresh box of gloves. "And of course you're going to want to make sure the sizes match. That's the most important part."

She watched as he attached a label.

"Very good," she said. "Now if you can just do them all like that we'll be in great shape." She grabbed another box from the stockroom and placed it at his feet.

"Hey, Steve," ComicConQueen said. "Anything to add?"

"Band-Aids are in the medicine cabinet."

For those extra days, I brought my iPod loaded with interview-based podcasts. I listened to one of my favorite stand-up comedians talk about the fact that, even when he was selling out shows, he worried that he wasn't good enough. Rarely did I believe I'd ever break the cycle of temping and be able to financially support myself with my writing. It inspired a tweet I posted at the break—"If you've never felt like your art sucks, your art probably sucks."

After the job ended I paid off the first installment of my debt to the government and loaded my shelves with boxes of mac and cheese. It wasn't long before I was back in the same place I'd been when I turned down the copyediting job. Had I taken it, my bank account wouldn't have been so low that I couldn't meet the twenty dollar minimum to withdraw money from the ATM, but I could live with that just so long as I didn't have to put on the red light.

Christmas Cookies

When I was twelve years old, I shoveled driveways in the early weeks of winter to earn money to buy Christmas presents for my family. I decided that I was too old to give my mom a card made out of construction paper with a poorly drawn Santa Claus, and I could no longer get away with gifting my dad his own golf balls I'd stolen from his bag. My mom loved my sloppily decorated cards and put them on display above the fireplace until late spring, and my father appreciated the thought that went into my attempt at pawning off his personal belongings as a gift. But when my teens approached, I felt it was time I bought my family "real" presents.

I was proud on Christmas morning when I watched my mom open an eight-dollar bottle of perfume I bought at Canadian Tire.

"I think this is only for fancy occasions," she said.

My dad seemed pleased with his golf-club-shaped soap-on-a-rope, and by the way he said, "Well done, son" as he put it aside with his other gifts, I could tell he was more pleased about the fact that I'd learned a lesson about money than he was happy about a piece of soap that boasted a fresh pine scent.

When I went off to college, all the money I made from odd jobs went to late-night pizza orders and bags of weed and when school broke for winter break I was always broke. It was uncomfortable to be gifted thoughtfully chosen books from friends and family, only to give a mix CD or coupon for five free driveway shovelings in return.

The first job I had after college that required a degree was in the financial department of a nonprofit. It was a three-month contract with the possibility of an extension. Before that, I'd been bouncing between warehouses and service industry jobs, which always brought on embarrassment when someone asked me what I did. "I kind of write," I'd say. "Oh you mean, like, how do I pay the bills? I'm a pizza boy."

In addition to having a piece of paper from a four-year college, the only other skills listed in the job description were typing, filing, and label making. I checked the box next to all three of those talents when I registered with the temp agency, and my recruiter thought I was "perfect" for the position.

I accepted when I learned the job paid a few dollars more than what I averaged delivering pizza. Relying on tips made every check unpredictable, so I could never make plans based on future earnings. Knowing the amount of my paycheck at the end of every week meant there was potential to redeem myself for the previous five years of poor gift giving. It had gotten so bad that my parents put my name on presents for my nephew. I was happy to know he wasn't getting shortchanged because of a deadbeat uncle, but when my sister would tell him to thank me after unwrapping a present that was just as much of a surprise to me as it was to him, I felt a gut punch of shame.

Martha was in charge of organizing the books in preparation for the end of the year, and it was my job to assist her in tracking down financial records. Martha was in her mid-forties, had short hair that was more practical than stylish, and wore red and green sweaters with busy holiday designs that would kill at a hipster ugly-sweater party. Though she didn't appear to wear them "ironically." While she crunched numbers at her desk, she'd have me pull and file receipts from a long, waist-high cabinet that stretched through the center of the office. I spent all day kneeling on a worn beige carpet while reciting my ABCs in my head to figure out if "U" came before "V."

"Steven, I need quarter two records from the Johnson account," Martha would call out from her cubicle. I'd pull the appropriate manila folder and place it on the corner of her desk and then return to the stack that needed to be put away.

When Thanksgiving approached, cookies, cupcakes, and candies appeared on top of the filing cabinet. The festive spread was put together before my arrival, and I didn't know how it got there, but the diversity of the goods led me to believe it was a communal effort from the entire office. I wondered if there was a scheduled rotation and hoped temps weren't expected to contribute. Or at least I hoped my coworkers were judgmental enough to assume a guy in his twenties who only had two work shirts wouldn't know how to bake. They'd be correct. The best they could expect out of me was a sleeve of Chips Ahoy.

"Ooh, snickerdoodles," Martha said. "It is the holidays. Maybe just one." She had this debate with herself every morning, loud enough for me to hear, as though she believed I had a spreadsheet where I documented her daily caloric intake. After lunch she said things like "This is my last one, I promise," or "Nothing but kale for dinner tonight."

I never partook in the office treats, but didn't want Martha to think I was judging her, so I said things like "I had a really big breakfast" or "I already had one when you weren't looking."

"What do you have to worry about? Your metabolism is so good," she said while pushing a tray of brownies under my nose. "You're going to make me feel like a pig if you don't have at least one."

Her assumption that my thirty-inch waist was a result of genetic luck was false. She didn't know that my northern native Canadian roots were deep, and my ancestors sometimes went whole winters without food. I'd evolved to store fat like a walrus. One too many slices of pizza and I sprout man-boobs.

At the end of each day, she ordered me to take the leftovers home by saying, "You could use a little more meat on your bones." It was easy to say no to a plateful of sugar cookies during the day, but I knew I wouldn't have the same willpower home alone. I could destroy a whole plate of brownies during an episode of *The Simpsons*.

"No thanks, Martha," I said. "I'm not going home right after work so I wouldn't want it to go bad."

While I crawled around the cabinet pulling files, she told me about her diet plan for the new year.

"I'm going to have a second cookie today because come January first, it's no sugar for thirty days. Not even in my coffee."

I looked up and gave her a reassuring nod. "That's a good plan."

"How about you? Any plans for the new year?" she asked.

"I'd like to find a permanent job," I said and hoped she'd say something about the state of my contract.

"That's a good resolution," she said, but failed to recognize my hint.

I didn't love the job, but more importantly, I didn't hate it. The hours flew by as I filed endless stacks of carbon-copied donor receipts and thought about what I was going to write after clocking out. Six hours of filing may have been monotonous, but when I returned home I hadn't been stripped of my desire to create. And there was the added bonus that thirty hours of filing paid more than forty hours of pizza delivery.

A contract extension would provide financial security without sacrificing my writing time—two things I once believed to be mutually exclusive. I'd placed a few poems in unpaying journals that went largely unnoticed, but I aspired to one day find myself in a position where my writing paid the bills. Filing for six hours a day seemed like a low-stress way to make money until that happened.

Hoping to give Martha a reason to keep me around, I engaged in small talk with her, which mainly revolved around the artistic merits of the frosting design on a snow-man cookie or her son's indoor soccer team.

"He scored two goals last week."

"He must get his athletic skills from you," I said while looking up to her from the carpet.

"Certainly not from his father."

I didn't know how to respond and looked across the room as if I just noticed something important.

"He's got two left feet."

"Sure," I said, followed by a forced laugh. I turned my head toward her and noticed the absence of a wedding ring.

"Just because he gets to eat junk when he visits his dad, my son thinks he's some sort of hero." She reached over my head for a snowman cookie. She admired the delicate craftsmanship of the chocolate buttons that ran down its coat. "I don't allow junk in the house," she said, then bit off Frosty's head.

During the second week of December, Martha appointed me gatekeeper of the cookies and instructed me to only allow her two a day. Since food monitor wasn't listed in the original job description, I didn't take the responsibility seriously.

"I'm stress eating," she said. "Slap the food out of my hand if you have to."

If I noticed her eyeing the filing cabinet I pretended that I needed to use the bathroom, leaving the treats unguarded.

"I told you not to let me have a third," she said and threw the last bite of a brownie in her mouth.

"It's the holidays," I said.

When she asked about my Christmas plans, I thought she might be close to proposing a contract extension.

"Visiting family, but not long," I said. "I'll be back the day after Christmas."

"My kid will be with his dad, so I'll probably just volunteer at soup kitchen or something," she said.

Two weeks before Christmas, my mom called to tell me she had scheduled and paid for my flight to visit the family, and I asked her what was on everyone's Christmas list.

"Just getting to see you will be present enough."

Knowing I'd have some money, I pressed her for ideas and hoped to recapture that sense of pride I felt when I was twelve. She made her best attempts to dodge the question, but I persisted until she revealed that my nephew wanted a spaceship Lego set.

On the last day before holiday break, Martha took violent bites of her angel cookie by devouring the feet and wings before decapitation.

"He knew I was planning on getting him a bike," she said while aggressively chewing her cookie and spilling crumbs on the carpet next to the filing cabinet where I knelt all day. "He's such a jerk."

"You can still get him something cool," I said.

"Nothing's cooler than a bike."

I grabbed an angel cookie and flew it around the air toward my face, then sent it into my mouth.

"Merry Christmas," I said.

She let out a soft laugh. "That reminds me," she said. Her slight grin disappeared as quickly as it had formed. She played with a bell that dangled off the Christmas tree on her sweater. "You've been a great help." She reached for a sugar cookie shaped like a present and pointed it toward her mouth. "We're going to miss you around here."

"Thanks," I said.

A few days later I was sitting on the couch with my mom and sharing a plate of Nanaimo bars. Bing Crosby played, and a colorful Christmas tree displayed a lifetime of ornaments.

"Do you remember making that?" she pointed to a clay soccer ball on a low branch that hung from a fraying red ribbon.

"Not really," I said.

"It was the year you wanted Super Mario Brothers 2."

"I loved that game."

"It wasn't easy to get," she said and reached for a bar. "I had to preorder it and do some wheeling and dealing. It was the most popular gift that year."

I remembered my excitement that Christmas morning. After unwrapping the game, I ran off to play, even though I still had unopened presents. "I had no idea."

"Seeing how happy you were was worth it."

"I was happy," I said. "I hope I gave you something good that year."

"You did. That soccer ball hanging from the tree."

"Doesn't seem fair," I said. "It's not even well-crafted. You have to hang it from a bottom branch, and it's still struggling." The heavy ball of hardened clay dangled inches above the pile of presents. "I doubt you spent every waking moment, for six months, playing with that ball like I did playing that game."

"I've been enjoying it almost twenty years."

"I guess that's pretty cool," I said as I stared at the ornament gently hovering above a metallic green bow stuck to a present for my nephew. It had my name written on the card. "I haven't played Mario Bros in years."

"One day you might not be able to come home for Christmas and I'll have that to remind me of you."

"Hopefully, next year that won't be something you have to preorder. I'm sure I'll have a full-time job by then," I said, with a little bit of wishful thinking. I had no idea what my employment situation would be, but hoped if I didn't have anything going on, Martha would be happy to rehire me.

"Have another Nanaimo bar," my mom said. "It's the holidays."

Now for the Disappointing Part

Clenching every muscle I could, I found a small space near the wall where I stood on my toes. I was willing myself to be as thin and straight as possible. I didn't want to touch the dirty wall behind me or the sweaty man in front of me, and here in the group of twenty or so people, I hardly looked out of place. They ranged in age from just out of teendom to the upper edges of middle age, and, as if we could be an ad for the American dream, featured every color in the rainbow. Still, I felt like I didn't fit. Just a few months prior I was an account manager, sitting in a cushy office easily paying my bills and contributing to my 401(k). But that life was in the past, and every day I felt like I was further and further from returning to it.

I made sure not to get caught staring as I looked over each person, trying to determine what events had led them to this room. Two guys wore suits. A woman was in a dress and heels, which I thought was a bad choice. A number of men had on jeans and hoodies. One guy, wedged into the corner, wore blinding yellow Crocs. A man with long stringy white dreads opened and closed a Zippo lighter. I wore khakis and a button-up shirt I bought from Old Navy with a birthday gift card—underdressed compared to my normal job interview outfit, but slightly more professional than my typical T-shirt and jeans.

We had all responded to an open call for UPS holiday help. I was skeptical since nowhere in the job description was there a mention of the hourly wage. I told myself I'd accept anything above $14, which was a significant drop from the $20 an hour I had made at my previous job.

We were led into a large conference room and given a sheet of paper with the meeting's agenda. At the very end there was a bullet point that read "hours and pay."

"Before we get started does anyone have any questions?" the man at the head of the room asked. He was in charge of HR, and his toned biceps and thick neck gave the impression he had spent time hauling packages before working his way up to a desk job. "You over there," he said to a guy in the back.

"What's the pay?"

"I'll get to that," he said. "My name is Ron. I'm going to tell you about the driver helper position, and then we're going to do some one-on-one interviews." He tugged on a Seahawks lanyard hanging from his neck that displayed his name badge.

"This job isn't for everyone," he said and sized up his new batch of potential laborers. I had spent plenty of summers pushing lawn mowers and packing heavy things into trucks, but this was the first time the label *laborer* seemed appropriate for me.

"Feel free to get up and leave if you hear something about the job you're not comfortable with," Ron said. "I won't hold it against you. There's no point in sitting here if you're not right for the job."

I looked around the room and considered who would be the first person to leave. There was a woman who couldn't have been taller than five foot two and had thin wrists. Was she aware that all employees were required to be able to lift fifty pounds? Next to her was a man made of brick. His work boots and worn flannel shirt reminded me of the guys I used to see standing in front of Home Depot when I drove to the office. I imagined he'd be hired on the spot. I ranked somewhere between them. Fifty pounds wouldn't be a struggle, but I'd be sore the next day. I hadn't lifted much more than a coffee mug at my previous job.

"Don't enter a fenced-in yard if there's a barking dog," Ron said. His tone was professional and friendly. "Maybe if it's a little dog you can, but stay away from anything that looks like Cujo." He paused and a few people laughed. "Dress warm and don't distract the driver. And most importantly, handle packages with care. You never know when a camera is on you. I don't want to see any of you ending up on YouTube throwing a flat screen. It's not good for business."

The job sounded easy enough. I would be paired with a driver working in my neighborhood that would pick me up and drop me off near my apartment. However, I did worry about running into someone I knew. Getting caught in a stop-and-chat situation while assisting a UPS driver seemed like a surefire way to destroy the image I'd been trying to create—as someone who had his shit together. I was sure I'd be met with an encouraging tone if I was spotted by an acquaintance while on the job, but I knew I'd be regarded with pity. I imagined someone saying "Oh, you don't even get to drive the truck? You're, like, just a UPS man's assistant?" while I looked down. "Good for you."

My second concern came when we were told there was no set schedule. Driver helpers were on call, and the driver decided every morning whether he needed help or not. Helpers were to expect a call early in the morning if help was needed.

"Does this mean we shouldn't expect to work forty hours a week?" one of the suits asked.

"It all depends on how you and the driver click," Ron said. "If you go out on your first day and you vibe with your driver and he wants to pick you up every day until Christmas Eve, then you're all set. Other drivers won't require help every day."

"Full-time work isn't guaranteed?" the man asked. He was playing with the pocket of his suit, trying to pry open the flap. He gave up when he realized it was sewn shut.

"No, but it's a likely possibility. You wouldn't be here if it wasn't."

The guy in the suit stood, pushed in his chair, and exited the room.

Had it been my first month of unemployment I would have followed him out, but I had nothing to go home to. If not for that meeting, I would have never gotten out of bed that day. I spent most of my time alone in my apartment browsing the internet for fight videos. Watching a couple shirtless guys pound on each other behind a liquor store was the only thing that stopped my brain from panicking—that and competitive cooking shows.

At night, the glowing numbers on my digital clock manically danced at my bedside as I stared at the ceiling. It seemed unfair that keeping the roof over my head required finding a job whether the work stimulated me or not.

I was aware society would collapse if everyone only pursued passion projects because a world with more ventriloquists than vegetable pickers was not a better one. I just couldn't understand how a system based on majority rule could produce more unhappy people than happy people. It kept me up so late that it became early, and I heard my neighbors lock their doors as they left for work. I'm sure they agreed with me and probably had something they'd rather be doing instead of heading to their job, but the burden of debt caused them to believe that wasn't an option.

When the emptiness of the building echoed into my room, I'd wonder why I couldn't live like everyone else. *Maybe I'm not cut out for all this and I should call it quits*, I thought. I certainly wasn't brave or desperate enough to do anything drastic, but I fantasized about being an innocent victim of a mass shooting. It seemed like an easy way to change the public perception of me—an image of me in a tie taken from my LinkedIn profile would show up on the news during a report on an isolated white male who snapped. Instead of *unemployed loser* I'd be looked at as *heroic victim*.

"Now," Ron said tugging on his lanyard, "for the disappointing part."

The guy across from me who seemed to have checked out raised his head off the back of his chair. A girl who'd been texting sighed and slipped her phone into her purse.

Ron held a nervous smile as he told us we'd earn a little more than eleven dollars per hour. The group shrugged in unison. I caught eyes with a guy in a University of Washington sweater. He smirked and walked straight out the door. No one spoke, but the room was loud with movement. The last time I made that kind of money was working in my college library over a decade ago.

The other guy in a suit left. Someone in the back wearing pressed Dockers with white sneakers followed him. I shifted in my chair but thought *maybe I can still do this*. Or maybe I had to do this. I wasn't far from putting in a call to my dad to ask for a loan, something I hadn't done since graduating college, and I feared requesting a handout more than running up my credit card debt. Accepting his money was an admission of failure. When I'd crossed the stage and received my diploma, I never expected that ten years later I'd need his help, let alone consider a job that barely paid over minimum wage.

Yet I hadn't heard anything that was a deal breaker. I could work whenever I got called and continue my job search. If something better came along I'd stop answering my phone.

"Okay, you guys have all had enough of me," Ron said. "I'm going to hand the floor over to Tammy, who is a union representative."

Tammy was a stocky woman who looked like she had skin made of leather, which I assumed came from spending the last twenty years of her life in a boys' club. "Who knows why it's a good thing to join a union?" she asked.

Looking around the room and judging by the puzzled faces, I wasn't the only one curious as to why a union rep was here for a job that was only one month long. When no one attempted to answer her question, she continued.

"A career at UPS can help you raise a family and provide you with benefits, and certain positions even help pay for college. Have you ever noticed when you're at a party and someone says they work for UPS and everyone looks at them in awe, like, 'Damn you work for UPS?'"

I'd heard about the great benefits, but I'd never been at a party where the UPS man was looked at in *awe*. I met a FedEx guy at a party once, and no one seemed to pay him much attention until he shared a story about having sex in his truck.

"If you accept this job you will have to join the union," Tammy said. "Joining the union requires a $250 initiation fee. A percent labeled 'union fees' will be deducted from your paycheck. Once you have paid that off, you're in the union."

I stood up from my chair and headed toward the exit. As I passed Ron I shook his hand and thanked him for the opportunity. I took a look at the group before closing the door behind me. This time their clothes weren't what stood out to me. It was their faces. They looked worn out and sleep deprived, as if they had also spent the previous night wondering if they'd ever figure out how to fit into the system without compromising happiness. We were all there for the same reason. Yet, my circumstances were comfortable enough that I could walk out the door, which made my worries and moronic death fantasies seem less valid.

A few days later I noticed the UPS trucks driving around my neighborhood were carrying an extra person. On my way home from the bank where I'd just traded in a twenty-four-ounce cup of coins for forty-seven dollars in bills, I passed a helper on the sidewalk. I had to move out of his way since the box he was carrying was so large it obstructed his vision. When he got to the doorway, he lowered the package and tapped some numbers into the callbox. He glanced over his shoulder. His collar was wrinkled and sweat stained. I wasn't sure if we'd been in orientation together, but the look of tired fear that had been plastered across everyone's face in that room was not present on his, at least not then. He seemed almost to smile to himself as he waited for someone to answer the door.

"Here you go, sir," he said as he handed off the package. He ran back to the truck and grabbed another box. He tucked it under his arm and rushed off down the street. He had purpose. Something I hadn't had in months.

PART III

5:00 p.m.

At 4:40 you decide you're going to take the 4:57 bus home. Usually you take the 5:10, but today has been one of those days. You haven't done any work in the past twenty minutes and figure that, even if you stayed until the appropriate time, you would just flip through Reddit instead of working anyway. You shut down your computer and glance at the ring stain on your desk and make a mental note to clean it tomorrow.

Everyone has lined up along the sidewalk in single file. The bus hasn't come yet, but that's just what people do at this stop. You find the organization comforting. Today you're the sixth person in line, which means you can probably squeeze into a seat, but you're not much in the mood for sitting.

The bus pulls up to the curb. A biker in a DayGlo jacket loads his bike on the front of the bus, then cuts in front of you. You believe proper etiquette should be that he has to walk to the end of the line, but you don't say anything.

You make your way to the back and stand next to the door. Unlike the morning, you're not carrying your travel coffee mug, so you have a free hand. You pull your phone from your pocket and open up the Daily Solitaire challenge.

You've been playing for a year, but have yet to complete a full month—you tend to forget to play on weekends—you complete the round in two minutes and forty-eight seconds. It's an average time. Your best is a minute twenty-two. You spend the rest of the ride staring out the window thinking about what's in your fridge and your options for dinner.

When the bus arrives at your stop, you're the first one off and you power walk to your apartment. You jaywalk when the light takes too long and cut across the street when the woman walking a dog in front of you isn't moving fast enough. You already have your bag off when you walk through the front door. It takes a matter of seconds to peel off your work clothes and change into your running gear.

You strap an iPod to your arm, raise the volume to the max level, and you're back out the door. You're unsure how far you're going. That decision is made after you climb the set of eighty stairs at the one-mile mark. You've built up a lot of anxiety over the week and figure a long run is the only way to dispel it. Earlier in the day you found yourself on your ex's Facebook page analyzing her likes and recent friend additions. You assume she's moved on, and you're curious whom she's brought along for the ride. You're disgusted by your jealousy and hate yourself because you can't let go.

You reach the top of the stairs and feel calm for the first time all day as you exhale a silent scream. There's a bounce in your step, and you feel like you could run for hours as pieces of the day fall off with every stride.

You complete eight miles with an uphill sprint. When you return to your apartment, you take off your shirt and move the coffee table to the side of the room so you can lie out on the carpet. You look at the ceiling while pulling your legs to your chest, one at a time, focusing on your breathing. Your head is light, and you can feel the absence of anxiety. You're not quite content, but it's the best you're going to get.

You spend twice as long in the shower as you did in the morning and let the hot water wrap around your skin.

You throw on a pair of gym shorts and a hoodie and turn on the TV to a four-episode block of *Seinfeld* reruns. There's a Tupperware in the fridge filled with a mix of beef, onions, rice, beans, and green peppers you prepared over the weekend. You throw it in the pan and stir it while it heats up. When it's ready you spoon it into a flour tortilla with a heaping helping of lettuce that spills out the side when you roll it into a burrito. You eat it in front of the TV, where you pause every now and then to laugh at a joke you're hearing for the fourteenth time. George's parents are your favorite.

After washing the dishes, you bring your laptop to the couch. You check your email, then Twitter, then Reddit, then Facebook. It's your turn in Scrabble. You've been playing a regular game with your folks since they both joined Facebook four years earlier. Whoever drops the last tile starts the next game. You've lost track of how many you've won and lost, but know your dad is the champion. You play your turn and scan your feed. Nothing interesting.

You type the first initial of your ex's name in the search bar, and the rest auto-fills. Her relationship status hasn't changed. You know you shouldn't be doing this. You even ask yourself "what good can come of this?" before clicking on her pictures. Some guy has been throwing likes all over her albums, even commenting "cute" on a pic you took of her one night when you had dinner with her parents.

You prepare the following day's coffee, then flip through Netflix, trying to decide if you're going to watch a documentary about how all the food we eat is poison or an episode of *Law & Order*. You don't really care since you know you will most likely fall asleep before the final credits.

It's hard to say if you've seen this episode or not. You fall asleep to the show so often, it all feels familiar. It doesn't matter anyway because you drift off before Ice-T gets a chance to interview the second suspect.

At 1:00 a.m. you wake. You open Facebook. No new status updates. You go to the bathroom and open the medicine cabinet. You take a melatonin pill with a tall glass of water. As you put the bottle back, you see yourself in the mirror and notice a hole in the shoulder of your T-shirt. You return to bed and set the alarm for 5:00 a.m.

American Temp

Six months of unemployment ended when I got a call from a recruiter offering an Amazon contract for a seller support agent. I negotiated the pay three dollars higher than the original offer and said, "I'll take it" without bothering to ask "What is a seller support agent?"

Apparently it only takes three weeks of training to learn how to support Amazon sellers. If someone had a problem with a bad review, they called me. If they hadn't received payment for a product they already shipped out, they called me. If their account had been blocked or suspended, they called me. If they weren't happy with the amount they were charged in postage, they called me. Sometimes, if they were just kind of lonely and wanted to brag about how well they were selling on Amazon.com, they called me.

All my calls began with "Amazon seller support, this is Steven, can I please have the last four digits of your credit card or bank account?"

Most of the callers I spoke with had just spent ten minutes on the phone with a customer service agent located in one of Amazon's international call centers, and by the time they got to me, they'd already spelled out their email address at least twice in military call letters and were dying to speak to an American human. The most common first question was "Do you know English? Were you born here?" I'd give them a confident "Yup," to put them at ease.

Once the caller was confident English was my first language, they asked about their account. I'd put them on hold, telling them I "needed to do some research," which really meant popping my head over my cubicle wall to ask the girl next to me the same question. Ninety-nine percent of the time she knew the answer, told me, then I took the seller off hold and answered the question in what was apparently thought of as an acceptable American accent.

The girl on the other side of my cubicle wall was Ratna, a shy woman with a nervous smile, who dressed in sweaters from the young adult section at Macy's and had a thick Indian accent. We went through training together, and in a class of over twenty people, we were the only two who honestly expressed our anxieties at the thought of not being able to answer a customer's question.

She fought her anxiety by doing the best in training, making sure to learn everything so she'd never find herself in a situation where she'd be forced to say, "I don't know." I tried taking a similar approach, but I couldn't focus on the lessons. We were supposed to follow along in a training manual while everyone in the class took turns reading a paragraph. My already heightened anxiety was turned up to eleven because I was terrified of reading aloud. I'd never gotten over the time I read a chapter of *Hatchet* in fifth grade and pronounced "grimacing" as "garassing," and Darrin Peterson called me dyslexic for the rest of the year.

I found the easiest way to keep myself calm was to trade IMs with a cute chick who sat in the back row and make her "lol" with pictures of squirrels with their heads stuck in peanut butter jars or kittens dangling from ceiling fans. Other times I searched Amazon for authors I was envious of and read their one-star reviews.

Thankfully, Ratna was just a few inches of plywood away.

On a regular basis I got phone calls from sellers asking, "Why can't I sell a breast pump in the used section?" or "How come no one is buying my used copy of *The Da Vinci Code* that's priced at fifteen dollars?" Those were the easy questions to which I could answer, "Ma'am, you can't sell used products in the health category" and "The reason no one is buying your used copy of *The Da Vinci Code* is because others are selling it for one penny, so you might want to consider lowering your price." The questions that made me sweat were the ones about uploading giant inventory files or someone complaining about a policy violation, like how come they're not allowed to put their company address in their product picture. I'd kindly ask them to hold in a shaky voice and pop my head over the cubicle wall.

"Hey, Ratna, should a flat file be uploaded as XML or as an Excel spreadsheet?" I'd ask, or "What is the policy on directing customers to an external website?" Ratna always gave me an answer, and I appreciated that she never seemed bothered when I asked for help. "You're welcome, Steven," she said with a smile at the end of our interactions. Occasionally she asked me a question, but I was rarely helpful. Usually I'd just smile and shake my head while mouthing the word "sorry."

"Thanks anyway, Steven. I will just consult my notes."

We each had our own five-by-five-by-five cage with two computer screens and a headset. There was a fifteen-minute break in the morning, sixty minutes for lunch, and another fifteen-minute break in the afternoon. Ratna and I never hung out during those moments of free time, mainly because I was shy, awkward, and terrible at small talk, but more than that, because she wasn't a smoker. The rest of the tar bar swingers and I hung out in the parking lot, where we avoided eye contact and made occasional remarks on the weather. On really bad days, when something was wrong with the system and calls were heightened and people treated us with even less respect than usual, we didn't even stand near each other. I'd hide in the corner sucking on a cigarette, while hoping for a massive power failure or some type of natural disaster that would force the workday to end early.

Ratna spent her off time at a table in the break room reading a book with a look of contentment on her face, like she was enjoying the silence more than I would ever understand.

When I received a call it meant the person on the other line had been unsuccessful in solving their problem independently and had no other option except calling me. They were frustrated and expected immediate resolution, and if they didn't sense that coming, they attacked.

What I lacked in knowledge I made up for with a friendly attitude and the ability to not take anything too personally. Regularly being called an idiot was a main component of customer service. A woman who sounded like my grandmother said I was dumb as a bag of rocks because I didn't know the shipping cost of a seven-ounce jar of maraschino cherries. I often had calls begin with "Are you going to be able to fucking help me," before I even knew what the problem was. "Your issue is important to me. I'm here to help," I'd respond. I could usually convince the caller that I deeply cared about their problem and would do everything in my power to resolve it.

Other times there was nothing I could say because there was nothing I could do. If a small business owner lost five hundred dollars on a deal gone wrong, I directed them to a website where they could submit their claim. I hated doing that because they were looking to me for salvation, and all I could say was "There's nothing I can do, but I understand your frustration." They got even more upset when I told them the claims department could only be reached through email. Then I would have to tell them to wait three to five business days for a response, and that was about the time I was told to go fuck someone or suck something and/or shove something up my ass. I laughed off the abuse by knowing I'd have a story to tell at the bar. Ratna couldn't shake off the insults as easily.

Regularly, I heard Ratna say, in her thick Indian accent, "No, sir, I'm in Seattle." One time she even followed up with "Matt Hasselbeck." I can only imagine that she was speaking to some redneck in a recliner chair with Cheeto crumbs on his chin, who asked, "If you're really in Seattle, who plays QB for the Seahawks?" One time a customer called her a bitch. I heard it shouted through her phone.

"Hey, are you okay?" I said while leaning over the cubicle wall.

"He was just angry," she said and tried to force her quivering lips into a smile. "I'm sure he's just upset about something else and took it out on me."

"Don't let some stranger get to you," I said. "Dude probably has a miserable life."

"His mommy probably never hugged him," she said, which morphed her false smile into something more genuine.

I thought maybe she'd be able to brush it off, but the next morning she didn't show up. Her cubicle was taken over by a recent college graduate who had no answers and pronounced the word "zero" like he was trying to shoot lasers out of his mouth.

Ratna's parents were not born in America, but she was. I was not. The callers who asked if I was born in the USA had a limited view of what being born in the USA meant, as if white people with TV-sitcom accents were the only true Americans. I'd lived in four major American cities, so I was familiar with the melting pot that is America, but I'd never experienced it like I did in phone support. I averaged twenty-five calls a day from all over America. I spoke with a wide range of nationalities. More often than not I was the one asking the customers to repeat themselves because I couldn't tell if they were saying "C" or "Z." It really would have been easier if everyone just said "zed." Sometimes I was told, "You speak English really well." I never knew if I should take that as a compliment or not. I do know it was better than the one time a girl told me I sounded like Napoleon Dynamite.

I'd lived in the States for over fifteen years and had yet to apply for citizenship. Presuming I didn't get caught committing a felony, my green card said I could stay the rest of my life. Just in case I snapped and knocked over a liquor store, I took note of a close female friend's childbearing hips, wondering, if the time came, would she be willing to carry my anchor baby? As a white, American-educated male with the ability to exaggerate my skills on a resume and the will to complete any assignment no matter how boring or tedious, I could reassure her I'd never go too long without a job. I had family and friends in Canada, but I didn't see myself ever moving back. I wouldn't even know where to look for work.

As a perpetual temp I moved from contract to contract, taking jobs from Americans while collecting unemployment in between gigs. Canadians are always overlooked in the immigration debate, maybe because we blend in so well. I've never once been pulled over and had my residency status called into question. Most immigrants are doing the jobs Americans don't want. Canadians are taking the jobs Americans do want. I know plenty of Americans who want Jim Carrey's job, but none who want Jamie Chavez's job picking tobacco under the North Carolina sun for three bucks an hour. And I highly doubt there are many Americans who want to bike in the rain to deliver General Tso's chicken and egg rolls. When I hear Republicans complaining about immigrants taking American jobs, I feel excluded.

I didn't know for sure, but there was a strong possibility I was paid more than Ratna. Equal work didn't mean equal pay in the temp world, which is why I never divulged the number on my paycheck. Some of my naive coworkers weren't aware of the wage gap and spoke freely about how much they were paid. When a fellow temp said, "This job isn't worth fourteen bucks an hour" after sharing a story about a customer who suggested he stick his head in an oven, I nodded in agreement. Canadians need to be liked, and I'm sure if he knew I was making three dollars more an hour for the exact same work, he'd resent me. Neither of us had worked in phone support, but I had more overall job experience because I was six years older than he was.

Usually by the time a person is thirty years old, they've settled on a career. Living in America allowed me to coast. I worked strictly to pay bills. When I walked out of the office at 5:00 p.m., all was forgotten until my return the following day. I'm sure I could have done the same thing in Canada, which is probably why Canadians are always overlooked. It's more of a lateral move when a Canadian shows up in America, as opposed to the wealth of opportunity it offers someone from a country where clean water is a luxury.

I came to the States in 1993 with my family in my father's pursuit of the American dream. IBM transferred him from Toronto to Connecticut so he could act as liaison between IBM America and IBM Latin America. My father is the first in his family to graduate high school as well as college. He's completely self-made and one of the smartest people I know.

However, he doesn't speak Spanish. It's ridiculous if you think about it—my father, a Canadian, immigrated to America to be a liaison between IBM America and IBM Latin America. I am happy my father got the job; it provided me with a privileged life, but it seems impossible that of the 387.5 million people living in South America and the 318.9 million people in the United States, there was not one bilingual businessman with better qualifications than a Canadian.

I knew the Amazon job would have been a hell of a lot easier if I spoke Spanish. Knowing the language would open up a whole world of American jobs for me. There'd been a number of times when I thought I found the perfect copy-writing job only to reach the end of the description and see "fluency in Spanish required." I had exaggerated on applications before, but I doubted I'd be able to pass as fluent when my only background was a C in Spanish 101.

There was nothing about the Amazon job that related to what I hoped to one day find in a career, but after six months of unemployment, I was happy for the work. Plus, I believed there was valuable life experience in phone support. My Canadian politeness had always been extended to customer service agents, but after being one, I treated them so nicely they probably thought I was stoned. I bet Ratna felt the same way at one point. I never learned why she stopped showing up. I assumed she'd quit, but hoped it was because she'd found a better job.

A few months after the contract ended, my parents stopped in Seattle on a drive up to British Columbia. They regularly returned to Canada to visit family and friends, but like me, had no plans of moving back permanently.

During their stay we went to a restaurant I'd never have been able to afford on my own. My father ordered a plate of freshly caught scallops and then brought up tattoos. He was recently retired and was letting go of the business persona he had carried the previous forty years, which isn't to say he was a square, but career men of his generation didn't ink their bodies. Our food came, and the conversation transitioned into what type of job I was looking for.

"Something not too stressful," I said while holding my wine glass close to my lips. "I don't know." I took a sip. "Man, these scallops are good."

When we finished our food my dad ordered a round of aperitifs, and I excused myself to have a cigarette, not expecting my father to follow me outside.

"Your mom hates the idea, but I'm considering getting a tattoo on this trip," he said.

"Let's get matching maple leaf tattoos," I said.

"Not a bad idea, son," he responded.

We went back inside and took our seats. I assumed the tattoo conversation was just a result of too much wine and didn't expect him to follow up.

"I'm about 70 percent sure about doing that thing we talked about," he said after handing the bill to our waitress.

"What thing?" my mom asked.

"Nothing," my dad said.

I helped them find a cab and said I'd meet them for breakfast the following day.

I returned to my apartment and noticed a missed text from my dad that said, "I'm 100 percent sure."

The next morning over eggs and coffee my dad asked if I knew of a good tattoo shop. There were a ton of places on Capitol Hill, but because I didn't have any tattoos I wasn't sure which were good. I knew there was a place two doors down from where we were eating breakfast. I mentioned it like I knew what I was talking about, still not totally sure we were going to go through with it. We paid the check, then my mom walked to a bookstore. She wasn't thrilled about the plan, but she wasn't against it either.

"It's your bodies," she said in that way mothers do.

We walked into the tattoo shop, my father much more confident than I. An hour later we were both branded with the symbol of a country neither of us lived in, his on his bicep and mine on my inner forearm. I never had much interest in getting a tattoo because it was a lifelong commitment, but sharing the experience with my father felt like something I wouldn't regret.

For the rest of my life, every time I met someone new and reached out to shake their hand, they'd see the leaf, and I wouldn't blend in so well anymore.

If the day comes when I get my citizenship and I'm asked to raise my right hand to swear an oath to the United States of America, the leaf will be broadcast across the courtroom—not as a sign of protest or unconditional loyalty to Canada, but as a symbol of America, a place diverse in culture, full of the people with the freedom to act as polite or rude as they want to customer service agents.

Luxury Items

I went to high school with kids who carried credit cards without limits. They always had full tanks of gas in their brand new SUVs and money for milkshakes and chicken strips at the diner. They bought concert tickets and CDs without a second thought and never saw a credit card bill.

I was raised comfortable. I got new soccer cleats when I grew out of my old ones and a new sweater every winter. I had everything I needed. It was the things I didn't need that I had to acquire on my own.

During the summer of eighth grade, when all my friends picked out new mountain bikes without considering the cost, I struck up a deal with my parents. They bought me a two-hundred-dollar bike on the condition that I paid them back with chores. A record of my debt was stuck to the fridge, and my mom subtracted ten dollars every time I mowed the lawn and five dollars when I washed her car. It took the whole summer to climb out of debt.

At the time, I thought my parents were being wicked lame, but learning that you need to do stuff to get stuff was beneficial for my life as a temp. I evaluated every purchase by how much work was required to pay for it, to determine whether it was a luxury item or a necessity.

I was not a beer snob. I'd crush tall boys of PBR or if someone else was buying sip microbrewed milk stout, but when
I said I was bringing a twelve-pack to the party, you could
predict with 100 percent accuracy that I was showing up
with a box of Rainier under my arm.

Unlike the meticulous decision-making that went into
the purchase of pizza delivery—was I financially stable
enough to order a twenty-dollar dinner or was it more
responsible to just eat a five-dollar Digiorno?—Rainier
never felt like a downgrade the way a frozen pizza felt compared to delivery. "It's not delivery, it's Digiorno." *Yeah, no
shit.*

When my finances were steady and I still had a decent
amount of time left on a contract, I swapped the occasional
twelve-pack of Rainier for Moosehead. Seeing twelve green
bottles lined up on the bottom shelf of my fridge symbol-
ized success.

Lunch meat didn't have a Rainier beer equivalent, and
I was a sandwich snob. I'd rather starve than eat a turkey
sandwich made with the spotted beige cold cuts that hang
next to the hot dogs in the grocery store. The sliced-before-
your-eyes Boar's Head maple-smoked turkey was significantly more expensive than those slimy sheets packaged by
Oscar Mayer, but well worth it. I rationalized purchasing
the more expensive option because, while on contract, I ate
a turkey sandwich for lunch every single day. The twelve
dollars I spent on a pound for the week, plus the ten dollars'
worth of bread, mayo, and Swiss were cheaper than hitting
the food truck, making it a necessity while on contract.
When I was unemployed, it was an easy luxury to give up.

On the other hand, boxed mac and cheese was a staple of my diet both when I was working and when I was unemployed. I doubted that even the most financially troubled college student would call a ninety-nine-cent box of Kraft macaroni and cheese a luxury, but when the store brand was fifty cents cheaper and you hadn't received a pay check in four months and rent was due, those fifty cents determined whether you wore a clean shirt to your next interview.

I've been eating mac and cheese from the box as long as I can remember. My mom always had it on hand for nights when I was too picky to eat her casserole. When my friends and I gathered in the kitchen after a day of street hockey, I'd whip up a batch. I ate it after high school while watching *Yo! MTV Raps* and showed up at the beginning of every college semester with a Costco pack of eighteen that never lasted longer than the first two weeks. I ate it for breakfast to cure a hangover and ate it at three in the morning to prevent one. I ate it with hot sauce, ketchup, and, when I was feeling fancy, a handful of bread crumbs. No matter what my financial situation, I made sure there was a box on hand. It comforted me to know it was always an option. If some insane series of events made me a billionaire, I'd still make sure to throw a couple boxes in my grocery basket before checkout.

I couldn't tell the difference between the store brand and Kraft in a blind taste test, but when finances were up I always went with the blue box.

I didn't have the same brand loyalty for clothes as I did for boxed mac and cheese. My style of dress was casual and comfortable. I stuck to classics like jeans, T-shirts, and solid-color button-ups. I never rocked name brands, because paying an extra $50 for a man on a horse stitched into the pocket didn't seem worth it.

I bought a new work shirt at the start of each new contract, because I liked having a selection. I'd rather wear a button-up I'd outgrown than hear "hey, we're twinsies" when passing someone in the hall. I once kept my favorite navy blue checker-print in the closet for six months because a manager who ended every meeting by saying "cool beans" had the same one.

Just like I couldn't tell the difference between the name brand mac and cheese and the generic, I figured the world couldn't tell the difference between a $20 Old Navy button-up and an $80 one from Nordstrom. Old Navy designers were smart enough to know that no one wants to advertise they wear Old Navy and have kept the clothes free of logos. Not representing a name brand aligned with my aesthetic and it also made it easy to forget that the hour of work I did to pay for the shirt was more than a week's pay for the person who made it.

I was only frivolous when it came to books. I got the same amount of pleasure from owning them as I did from reading them, and as a former English major I was conditioned to highlight passages and make notes in the margin. I loved that two years after reading a book I could pick it up and flip to a passage that moved me enough to underline it. Or when I read a great book that I knew a friend would enjoy, I liked that I could pull it from my shelf to share.

There was always something in my Powell's online shopping cart. When I read a review about a new rock-and-roll memoir that looked interesting or I found out that my favorite author released a new book, I'd add it to my cart. My bookshelf was plentiful and I had enough unread books to last me a year, which is why I never checked out my cart when I was unemployed. I'd stop adding once my total was over fifty dollars, because that's the minimum amount you need to spend for free shipping. (Everyone should do this instead of buying from Amazon.) On a break from searching job sites, I'd find myself browsing through my cart and looking forward to the day when those beautiful books would show up at my front door and I'd be faced with the difficult yet satisfying task of deciding what to read first.

Books were the only items I purchased when I had perfectly good, unused options on hand. Even when I was in the sweet spot, where I regularly added to my savings and 401(k) and had six months left on my contract, I never replaced something as long as it was working.

I was thirty-five years old when I bought bedsheets for the first time. I'd lived my adult life with two sets and never felt the need to replace them. I had one set of flannel sheets that I'd pilfered from my parents' closet when I was a senior in college and a cotton set my mom sent Ashley and me when we moved into our first apartment. I used the flannel ones in the colder months and the cotton ones during the rest of the year. I washed them on a fairly regular basis and ignored the fact that the pillowcases didn't match. One of the cotton cases had been ruined when Ashley and I brought a bottle of merlot to bed. I replaced it with a *Star Wars* pillowcase I'd had since I was five.

I didn't see a reason to spend money on something I already owned, until one night when I couldn't sleep. I rolled around the rough sheets like I had been for the previous two months and realized that I deserved better. I was making the highest hourly wage of my life and still had eight months remaining on my contract. Earlier that night I'd signed a forty-dollar bar tab without giving it a second thought, yet I deprived myself of new sheets because it seemed like a waste of money.

I did the math and decided that $34.99 for a set of jersey sheets was a viable investment. I would use them every day for at least half the year and figured the long run cost was twenty cents a day for the first year, and nothing but profit after that was worth it.

With soft sheets draped across my chest, it dawned on me that I'd lowered my quality of life just because I didn't think a necessity ever needed to be replaced.

I thought about the can opener with a broken handle that pinched my skin. For two years I'd dreaded making tuna sandwiches because preparation risked slicing my palm. It worked though, so I didn't see a reason to spend six bucks on a new one. Not until experiencing the joys of comfortable sheets.

When I got to the kitchen section of Target and saw all the things I could upgrade in my apartment, I turned into P. Diddy *tryna blow a check*. I threw a can opener with reinforced grips in my basket, then grabbed a nonstick spatula to replace the one I'd accidentally acquired from a roommate when I was nineteen. I got a kitchen towel, so I'd no longer have to walk to the bathroom every time I needed to dry my hands, and bought a small pot for all the cans of soup I now felt comfortable buying because the can opener situation had been resolved. The total came to twenty-five dollars, and I was much happier in the kitchen.

In high school, my friends and I would go to the mall when we had nothing better to do. We passed the time flipping through band T-shirts and baseball caps. I only browsed while they bought things without the thought of whether the purchase was a necessity or a luxury item.

Living with my parents meant all my basic necessities were taken care of, but spending the money I made from after-school jobs still required budgeting. When my friends wanted to stop at the diner before the record store I had to decide between eating and buying a CD. Knowing there would always be boxes of mac and cheese back at my parents' place, I always opted for the CD. I could enjoy music much longer than a meal.

My friends threw back milk shakes and bacon cheeseburgers while I drank water with quiet excitement and thought about all the possible discoveries I might encounter in the import bin. Knowing that buying a plate of chicken strips could jeopardize my chance of affording a Clash import made the tired lemon floating at the top of my glass of water refreshing.

In eighth grade my parents could have easily bought me a new bike without putting a dent in their finances, but they didn't. They wanted to teach me the most basic lesson when it came to money. If you want something, you have to work for it. It's like they knew my adult life would be one of unpredictable finances and wanted to make sure I was prepared.

I would have missed out that summer if I didn't have a bike. Whether it was a ride to a girl's house whose parents weren't home or a race through the trails, all plans started on bikes. I wouldn't have been able to keep up without one and would have spent that summer alone, which I guess meant it was a necessity.

Thinking about Thumbs

During a conversation about improving the user experience, I look at the person speaking and remember that she was once a baby with tiny thumbs. She cried when needing to be fed, changed, or held. I hear her voice, but there are no words. Everything's a wash, like waves crashing against rock. And it all falls into perspective. As if my whole life I've been looking at the world through a coffee straw and then, out of nowhere, the straw is pulled away, and I catch a glimpse of everything. The world, the past, the present, all of it—including me, an insignificant speck, who, somehow, came into being after billions of years of evolution and a precise line of consummation that eventually lead to this moment.

The last time I peeked at the universe like this it was 6:30 a.m. and I was waiting for the bus. I was pressed against a brick wall and trying to hide from the rain under the six-inch gutter jutting out from the top of the building. It wasn't enough. The gutter acted as a funnel, streaming water off the building onto my neck and down into my jacket.

I looked over at the hooded girl next to me. She didn't appear bothered by the weather. She rapidly thumbed at her phone, apparently unconcerned when a fat raindrop exploded on the screen. I was in awe of the controlled chaos that was her thumbs tapping at the keys. I found it beautiful, like ballet, but then felt silly for thinking that.

My mind opened up and it occurred to me that there was a fifth digit on my hand, set lower and opposable, and that I was waiting for a giant metal box on wheels, which ran on decomposed organisms that died long before my oldest ancestor crawled out of the ocean.

I suppressed these obvious observations, or else I'd act on instinct alone and try to initiate sex with strangers at bus stops. Instead I allowed myself to be punished by the weather, waiting to be carted off to a precise stack of stones, to spend the best hours of the day convincing myself that I was important.

These flashes never last longer than a moment or else I would be paralyzed with panic by calculating every experience and judging its value, knowing that I don't know when I'll return to the nothingness from which I came, tortured with guilt for each second I didn't take advantage of on a rainy Seattle day.

The bus arrived, and I followed the texting girl onboard. We both stood in the back, and she continued thumbing those keys. But the moment had passed. It no longer looked like ballet, and the bus was just a bus.

Five Types of Temps

The Full-of-Hope Temp

I worked with Hair Gel on an Amazon contract I accepted at a time when my finances didn't allow me to be choosy with employment. The position was a step backward for me in terms of pay and responsibility, but for Hair Gel it was the first step toward the American Dream. He was fresh out of college and parted his hair on a razor sharp line that was held fast with a glossy coating of what I imagined came in a sleek silver container and was referred to as *product*.

We met in the lobby on our first day, and I took a deep breath before revealing it was my fourth contract in four years.

"That's cool," he said without realizing I was ashamed of my circumstances.

He saw value in my experience and wanted to learn from a veteran who'd survive multiple tours of combat. He asked about the process of moving from temp to full-time employee.

"Buddy up with management and look for opportunities to improve workflow," I advised.

Two days later I saw him in the break room nodding enthusiastically at a manager's detailed description of a video game character he had created.

The work was frustrating because procedure was constantly changing. Regular tweaks to the system were an attempt to improve productivity, but having to learn new guidelines once a month made it difficult for some temps to get comfortable with the tools. I anticipated the changes, as it had been the case with every other Amazon contract I'd done, and adapted quickly. Hair Gel had a difficult time keeping up. Looking for a little guidance, he moved to an unoccupied desk to be closer to more experienced temps who could assist him.

The video-game-character-creating manager discovered the move and marched into our office red-faced.

"Why the hell are you here?" he said. The ambient keyboard chatter paused.

"I just thought I'd work better in here since these guys can help me if I have a question."

"That's not how it works," he said.

"Sorry, I just wanted to make sure I was doing a good job."

"We have assigned seats for a reason." He pointed to the door. "Go back to your desk."

Hair Gel collected his things and stared at the carpet as he exited the room.

"People," video-game-character-creating manager said. "If assigned seats weren't important, we wouldn't have them." He spun on his heel and exited the room, leaving behind a thick cloud of negativity that took thirty minutes to evaporate.

After being publicly humiliated, Hair Gel lost interest in my workplace wisdom. Instead, he asked me about Seattle's nightlife, which he was discovering for the first time. He wanted to know the best places to get a cheap shot of whiskey and what bars had the best happy hour. His questions made me feel old because all the spots I'd frequented at his age were gone. Instead of tips, I shared nostalgic stories about the good old days of Capitol Hill, when you could get a stiff whiskey ginger at the Jade Pagoda for a buck-fifty and the patio at Linda's was the best place to be on a summer afternoon. Having heard similar stories ten years prior about Charlie's losing its charm after the smoking ban and how the Roanoke was overrun by hipsters, I worried I bored him, but he seemed genuinely interested and asked questions like "Was the old Comet as cool as everyone says?"

During the second month, mandatory overtime was implemented, requiring us to work weekends. Hair Gel showed up that first Saturday sweaty and blurry-eyed. He spent the day fidgeting in his chair while sucking down Gatorade. The aura of ambition that had surrounded him on that first day in the lobby was gone.

One Tuesday he called in sick to drop ecstasy at the beach. Oh, to be young again.

Hair Gel noticed that I was absent on mandatory Saturdays and asked me how I pulled it off.

"I babysit my nephew," I said.

"I thought you didn't have any family in Seattle?" he questioned, referencing an earlier conversation we had one afternoon when we were supposed to be reviewing a new systems of practice document.

"I don't. My nephew lives in Arizona," I said while smiling. "This place doesn't dictate my weekends."

"I see," he said and leaned back in his chair. "Good excuse."

"Overtime pay is great and worth taking advantage of, but it's best to always have an excuse chambered," I said. "If there's an advantage to temping, it's that you don't owe the company anything outside of forty hours a week."

"Even when they say it's mandatory?"

"They can't force me to work on a Saturday and leave my nephew home alone. That's child endangerment."

He laughed, but didn't seem convinced.

"Think about it," I said. "If work is so busy they have to institute mandatory overtime, it's a result of being understaffed. As long as you're a good worker, they're not going to sacrifice letting you go because you missed a few Saturdays."

"Good point."

I'm not sure how much of his interest in my experience was genuine and how much of it was just small talk, but I enjoyed showing him the ropes. Besides his liberal use of hair gel, he reminded me a lot of myself at his age. Although I didn't have a mentor giving me tips on my first job. It wasn't until my third contract that I learned it was best to always have an excuse chambered. Of all the advice

I gave him, I hope that was something he held onto. When you're temporary, nothing should be mandatory.

The Let's-Be-Friends Temp

Black Hoodie was the type of guy you felt bad for not liking. He was friendly, never bothered anyone with annoying questions, and shared his mints at meetings. For an eleven-month contract, he wore the same black hoodie every day, which somehow never appeared dirty—maybe he had a bunch of them. Within an hour after meeting him, he friend requested me on Facebook, which I found peculiar because I'd already forgotten his name, yet he knew my first and last.

It was hard to say why I didn't like him, even after he picked up on that fact and was cordial enough to leave me alone in the break room and stopped asking about my weekend on Monday morning. He was a solid worker and was eager to help the less informed, but it only took one time for someone to learn that asking him a question, no matter how small, always resulted in a ten-minute interaction.

"Do you know how to print?" a young girl asked on her first day.

"Yeah," Black Hoodie said. He leaned over her shoulder and pointed to an icon in the corner of her screen. "Open that up." He moved his hand closer to her monitor and pressed his finger against the screen. "Just click that," he said.

She dragged her cursor under the greasy fingerprint he left behind and hit the button.

"Follow me." He escorted her across the office to the supply room that housed the printer.

"Where did you work before this?" he asked.

"Google," she said.

"Cool!" he said with an embarrassing amount of enthusiasm. "Did you know Google is actually a typo? It was supposed to be Goggle, but someone spelled it wrong and they decided to go with it."

"Neat," she said.

"It is neat, isn't it?"

He stood next to her as she waited for the printer to spit out her work. Her discomfort went unnoticed, and he continued interrogating her about her previous job.

"Was it a fun office?"

"I guess."

"We like to have fun here. You should come with us to happy hour."

"Do you do that regularly?"

"Kind of. Well, we haven't yet, but it's in the works. I'll send you an invite."

She retrieved the document, and he followed her back to her desk.

"The break room gets pretty busy at noon," he said. "That's why I eat lunch at 11:30."

"Cool." She turned to face her computer screen. The fingerprint had dried, but its impression remained.

"You should join me."

"We'll see," she said. He watched along as she opened her email. She glanced over her shoulder and stared at him until he turned and returned to his desk.

Every Tuesday morning, in hopes of finding four people to form a pub trivia team, Black Hoodie sent out a team-wide email with the subject line "Let's be nerdy and drink beers." He'd follow up later in the day with ideas for team names like "The Rubix Cubicles" or "The Nine to Fivers."

I enjoyed pub trivia, but never responded. I feared I'd be the only one to show and couldn't risk being stuck in one of his meandering stories. In an early training session, he took a seat next to me. As we waited for it to get started, he told me a drawn-out story about returning a pair of pants to Target. There wasn't even a payoff or an obstacle he had to overcome to return the pants. He just told me the details of waking up one Saturday morning and driving to Target to return a pair of pants that were too short. Traffic was good, and the exchange went flawlessly. I couldn't figure out why he felt it was an interesting experience to share.

My coworkers must have had similar experiences because, by the end of the second week, no one sat next to him in meetings, and when he pulled out his tin of mints, everyone avoided eye contact.

Our thirty-person team only met as a group for one hour a week. A manager reviewed procedure and common mistakes using a PowerPoint presentation accessorized with generic clip art. It seemed like a playful attempt at ironic humor to liven up dry header text like "Things to Keep in Mind When Saving a Document." It was an admirable attempt to make something as boring as how to title a spreadsheet fun, but the comic relief was mostly unappreciated.

"That's so good," Black Hoodie said as he banged his fist against the table and looked at a cartoon image of a cat with stars in its eyes.

"Seemed appropriate to go next to the part about never using capital letters in your titles," the manager said. "I know I will feel like that cat if the next time I open the share, everything is correctly named."

"Classic," Black Hoodie said.

Outside of the one weekly meeting, we were each confined to our own cubicle on a floor that housed hundreds. The job was demanding, and everyone had seen enough temps get canned when they couldn't keep up that there wasn't much interest in socializing. Awkward smiles occurred in the coffee line, and occasionally there was a mention of last night's game, but everyone's main focus was doing their time as painlessly as possible, so they could return to their real lives.

On the last day of his contract, Black Hoodie emailed the team details about his personally planned good-bye party at a bar a few blocks from the office. Since he'd been courteous enough to not engage with me upon realizing my disinterest, I didn't expect my attendance would be missed. I almost reconsidered because it was sad to think of him sitting at the bar alone with a pitcher of beer and three empty glasses across from him, but meeting up would have conflicted with my plans of spending the evening flipping channels and surfing the web.

Later that night I was scrolling through Facebook when I saw his latest status update.

Gonna miss all the rad folks I worked with. Hope we can work together again sometime!

The Full-of-Questions Temp

Buzz was a guy I worked with for three weeks on a cleanup contract at Amazon. A team of twenty temps was assembled to help with Amazon's absorption of IMDb.com. The task was to make sure all actors, directors, and writers had proper headshots when featured on Amazon's streaming video service. It was an easy job, and I almost felt guilty for getting twenty bucks an hour to essentially cut and paste.

I reviewed headshots and flagged any that didn't follow the proper guidelines. If an actor was missing a picture, I took a screenshot from a movie or TV show and uploaded it to IMDb. I often got distracted when I came across an interesting page. I'd fall into a rabbit hole, not realizing I just wasted twenty minutes reading Steven Seagal's "Did You Know" section. *He owns a large collection of guitars and samurai swords.*

"Hey, Steven," Buzz whispered, leaning over my shoulder. "Can an image be of a person when they're a child, but now they're an adult?"

To his credit our training wasn't much more than a quick rundown of guidelines by a temp who'd been hired two weeks prior to our arrival. Buzz's question hadn't been covered, but we had the same training, so I wasn't sure why he believed I knew more than he did.

"I don't know," I said.

He harmlessly buzzed from person to person with the mild annoyance of a fruit fly hovering over a bowl of bananas, asking questions no one could answer. The rest of the team didn't share his concern and made up their own rules whenever faced with something not covered in training. It was difficult to worry about mistakes knowing it was only a three-week assignment. We didn't even have proper workstations and moved between meeting and conference rooms, sometimes exceeding capacity, forcing some temps to work on the floor.

When we moved to a new conference room, Buzz made sure both of the women on our team had a seat before looking for his own. The rest of the team wasn't as courteous, often leaving Buzz to sit cross-legged against the wall.

While the rest of the team talked—complaining about the taste of the free coffee, sharing war stories of previous temp gigs, and making lunch plans—he stared at his computer with a confused crease across his forehead.

"Hey," I heard him say in his soft voice.

I leaned into my computer to give off the impression I was involved in something important, when actually I was reading trivia about the TV show *The Wire*. I'd ended up on the show page after following a trail of links that began with James Van Der Beek's headshot. *President Obama claims it's his favorite show, and Omar is his favorite character.*

"Hey," he said again.

"Huh," the guy next to me said.

"What should I do for someone like Ben Affleck? Sometimes he has a beard, and sometimes he doesn't. Should I take a picture with a beard?"

"Yeah, with a beard," the guy said.

"No," someone called out from the other side of the room. "It's like a passport photo. No facial hair allowed."

"That's not a rule," a different person said.

"He looks hot with a beard," one of the girls said, and the other nodded in agreement.

"So, I should go with a beard?" Buzz questioned.

I looked up from my screen and accidentally made eye contact with him. "I don't think it matters," I said. "Go no beard. His best role was O'Bannion in *Dazed and Confused*, and he's clean-shaven in that."

"Okay."

Unbeknown to us, there were contract extensions available for half the team. The managers who checked up on us every few hours were doing more than just making sure we hadn't burned the place down. They were compiling a list of temps competent enough to continue the job.

It was the afternoon of the final day when a manager came by and asked the guy sitting beside me to gather his things and go with him. I never saw him again. Ten minutes later another person was called, and the cycle continued. Had I known there was a reward for the last men standing I wouldn't have been so eager to get called. I assumed we were all cows headed for slaughter, and I wanted to take my spike through the brain as soon as possible to get it over with.

One by one the room emptied out, giving Buzz an opportunity to move from the floor to the table, where he continued working. The rest of us saw the future and abandoned work to browse the internet and send text messages.

"It was nice meeting you all," Buzz said after his name was called.

"Later," I said as the only one to respond.

When the manager returned, I hoped to hear my name. I was ready to accept my fate, like Schwarzenegger at the end of *Predator*—*a role he lost twenty-five pounds for*. I thought—*Do it! Kill me! Come on! Kill me now!*

But the manager didn't call anyone's name and sat down at the table with us. "We're happy with your performance and would like you to stay for another three months."

I later found out that there'd been an *Animal House*–style judging of the team. Our badge photos were projected on a screen in a conference room full of managers who assessed each temp's value. I understood why Buzz didn't make the cut. Personality goes a long way on a job that requires little skill, but I still found it odd he was let go. I bet, at the end of the three weeks, he had fewer mistakes in his work than anyone else on the team.

The Overlooked Temp

AC/DC was not your typical temp. He was fifty years old and had never spent time in an office. He worked construction his whole life, until a back injury made it impossible for him to spend a day on a job site banging nails and hauling bricks. He didn't possess the required bachelor's degree needed for the job, but had a cousin on the inside who pulled some strings.

He tucked his graying mullet under a ball cap and seemed to have an endless supply of faded band T-shirts.

Unlike some of our coworkers, who bought faux-vintage Led Zeppelin shirts from Target, the wear on AC/DC's shirts was genuine.

We met in training, and I knew we'd get along because any guy who considered an AC/DC T-shirt business casual was cool. We sat next to each other and small-talked about classic rock during the downtime. He was out of his element and asked me a lot of questions, which I never found bothersome. He always seemed to already know the answer; he was just second-guessing himself.

Our previous jobs couldn't have been more different, but I related to him more than the college grads closer to my age who sucked up to management and used meetings as a platform to brag about their analytics.

AC/DC caught on to the job quickly, reversing our roles of question asker and question answerer. Anytime I was unsure of something, he'd consult his notes and set me straight.

Even though he looked like the type of guy who shouted "Free Bird" at concerts, he had the best work ethic on the team. I never once saw him checking Facebook or his personal email. From the time he sat down in the morning until leaving at the end of the day, he worked, and it was top-notch work at that.

Unfortunately, his dedication was never rewarded. Unlike me, he wanted more responsibility and took advantage of opportunities to showcase his capabilities. He designed a few workarounds that improved productivity and shared them with the team, but when he volunteered for extra work he was passed over for younger, less-qualified guys who wore collared shirts.

"I can't believe Bradley got that project and not me," AC/DC said.

"Maybe Bradley gives better HJs than you," I said.

"It pisses me off. My numbers are way higher than his."

"That's true, but it's not like it comes with a pay raise. Why would you even want the extra work?"

"For my resume. I need experience. I hope to find another office job when this contract ends."

"Right."

"What's the point of working my butt off if no one even cares?"

When new people joined the team, they quickly realized AC/DC was the best person to go to for questions. Not only did he always have an answer, but he didn't make anyone feel like they were putting him out by asking for help—unlike Bradley, who managed to turn something as insignificant as misnaming a file into a crisis that warranted a team-wide email on the importance of file labeling.

Managers instructed new employees to direct all their questions to Bradley, but once they discovered how much of a hassle it was to talk to him, they chose to go to AC/DC instead.

Toward the end of AC/DC's contract, it was announced there was an opening for a team supervisor, and everyone was eligible to apply. A select few would be asked to interview.

The following day, AC/DC showed up without his hat and wore an unbuttoned collared shirt over a gray T-shirt. He looked uncomfortable, like a freshman at his first homecoming dance.

"Are you going to apply for the supervisor position?" he asked me.

"I think so, just because I feel like I should, but I'm not sure I want it."

"I hope to at least get an interview."

"There's no question you'll be called in to interview," I said. "You're the Bon Scott of this team."

"Dead?"

"Whoops, I mean Brian Johnson."

"I'd rather be Malcolm. He rips on guitar, but isn't too flashy about it."

"Whoever you are, you've proven to be the best person for the job. I hope you get it so you can continue down this highway to hell."

"Thanks."

As the days led up to the announcement of who would be granted interviews, the gossip among the temps was that AC/DC was the best person for the job. It's rare for such a unified belief when it comes to office politics, but AC/DC was unanimously liked. He was helpful, his work never needed to be reviewed, he only spoke in meetings when he had something worthwhile to contribute, and his age made everyone give him a little more respect than their peers.

I was relieved when I received notice that I would not be asked to interview for the position. I had no interest in the job, but when I told my dad about the opening, he said it was an opportunity I'd be silly not to take advantage of. Now I could tell him I tried, but they didn't want me.

"Got denied from the interview," I said to AC/DC. "They must not be interested in hiring an average employee who doesn't care if the company succeeds or fails." I expected AC/DC to laugh. He didn't.

"I got denied too," he said.

"Bullshit," I said, expecting him to follow up with a *gotcha.*

"It's true. They said I'm not eligible because I only have an associate's degree."

"So what? You've proven you know everything about the job and can train new employees."

"Doesn't matter. I don't have that piece of paper."

AC/DC played out the rest of his contract with the same hard-working attitude he'd shown day one. On his final day we didn't make false promises to meet up for a beer or even connect on social media.

"Good luck," I said as he prepared to hand in his laptop and badge.

"Thanks."

"It's a long way to the top when you want to rock and roll."

The No-Fucks-to-Give Temp

Hipster Doofus was one of those rare Canadians I met in the States whom I didn't like. Usually, when I ran into a fellow Canadian on foreign soil, we immediately hit it off. No matter how different we were, the common ground of being expats was enough to build a relationship. Unfortunately, I couldn't form that bond with Hipster Doofus. There was no aspect of his personality I found appealing. Canadians like him troubled me because every time he interacted with an American, he contradicted Canada's reputation for being likable and polite.

He responded to training with a very unCanadian-like arrogance by scanning his phone as our manager gave us step-by-step instructions on how to fulfill our new job duties. He dressed in a straight-off-the-rack hipster costume of flannel, skinny jeans, and black-framed glasses that felt contrived, as if this was a new look he was trying on for the first time. And his feeble effort at a beard was such a sad attempt at cool that I would have felt sorry for him had he not been tarnishing Canada's good name.

I was astonished that he'd openly watch Netflix on his assigned laptop and didn't show the slightest bit of concern when a manager walked by, not even minimizing the screen. I passed his desk on my way to fill up my water bottle, and he was engulfed in an episode of *Sons of Anarchy*.

He answered calls at his desk and spoke loud enough so everyone could hear. "Yeah, I'm supposed to be working right now," he said. "But I'm not. Everyone else is though."

When it was revealed that he hadn't been following directions and skipped important steps, it fell to the rest of the team to correct his errors. People who hadn't formed an opinion on him now hated him, and I feared that meant also hating Canada.

"Did you get that?" someone asked him after a training session on a new program. "Or are we going to have to fix all your fuckups in two weeks?"

"I've got it covered," Hipster Doofus said.

"Let's hope, Canada boy."

It would seem that after being called out for his errors, Hipster Doofus would have been more cautious with his work, but he wasn't fazed. He showed no remorse that he'd caused his coworkers extra work. He didn't even throw out an insincere "sorry." A Canadian that doesn't say "sorry" is like a leopard without spots. You don't believe one exists unless you witness one with your own eyes. And even then, you wonder if a spotless leopard could still be called a leopard.

His mistakes got so bad that two people were assigned to check his work. And as though he lacked the gene that produced humility, he continued to openly watch Netflix, moving on to *Dexter* after completing *Sons of Anarchy*.

When our contracts ended we banked the same amount of hours and earned the same amount of money, yet I completed twice the work he'd done with far fewer errors. While I stressed over meeting metric goals, he caught up on shows I could never find the time to watch.

I can't deny that I was jealous of the way he lived those five months. I could never just let go of all my fucks like him. No matter how awful the job, I always maintained some sort of care, even if that care was just to make sure I looked busy. I snuck in the occasional YouTube video every now and then, but nothing longer than two minutes, and I'd always give enough of a fuck to at least hide my screen when a manager was near.

He had no fear, and I guess it could be said that was an aspect of his personality I did find appealing—at least in the way outlaw bikers or morally cautious serial killers are appealing. If Hipster Doofus's give-no-fucks attitude hadn't been scarring Canada's reputation, I probably would have called him My Hero.

Black Eyes, Full Heart

I've never taken a good ID photo. My crooked smile always looks forced, and my nose crinkles as if I'd just caught a whiff of a forgotten gym bag. Knowing the first task of any new contract was to secure a photo ID, I'd wear my nicest shirt and make sure my hair was relatively combed. I'd hope to pull off something that looked distinguished, with a hint of playful charm—something like a Jonathan Franzen author photo—but always ended up looking like a high school yearbook reject. If the line wasn't too long, the photographer would offer a reshoot, which I'd turn down so as not to appear vain, even though I knew I was committing to an avatar that would be attached to every email and IM I'd send for the duration of the contract.

The weekend before my first day in Amazon's FBA Ops department, I tried impressing my girlfriend, Melissa, with a double flip off a high dive. We'd just spent the evening drinking pitchers in a karaoke bar until last call. I didn't sing, but I loved watching her. She brought the house down with "What's Up" by 4 Non Blondes. It suited her voice, and she committed to the "hey, hey, hey, hey" chorus, causing the bar to shake in applause. She glowed while walking through a crowd of people patting her on the back and saying things like "You killed it, girl!"

"Amazing as always," I said as she sat down next to me. I put my arm around her, and she leaned her head into me.

"I'm glad you liked it."

When the bar closed we walked across the street to the beach. I stripped down to my boxers, leaving my clothes in a trail behind me, not worrying about my wallet or phone. I swam out to a floating raft with two diving boards. When I was twelve my flips garnered attention at the public pool, but it had been ten years since I'd launched myself off a high dive. I got comfortable with a few angular swan dives and let my long body hang in the moonlight before splashing into the soberingly cold water.

I stood on the high dive and looked over at Melissa sitting at the edge of the water with my belongings in a neat pile next to her. It was too dark to make out her face, but it seemed as though she were watching me. I strutted across the board like Greg Louganis, then double bounced myself into the air. I tucked into a flip and rotated once, then another time, and kept going until I smacked my face against the water. As I sank to the bottom, the cold water numbed my face.

"Did you see that?" I asked Melissa as I pulled my sopping boxers up my waist.

"See what?"

"I just triple lindy'ed that shit."

"I got you a towel."

"Thanks. From where?"

"I ran back to my apartment. I didn't want you to freeze."

The following morning my attempt at showing off was displayed on my face. Blood vessels surrounding both pupils were broken, and puffy purple sacks hung under each eye. I looked like I'd just been peeled of a sticky fight club floor.

"Oh my," Melissa said when I slipped back into bed with her. "Your face."

"Is it really that bad?"

She put her hands on my cheeks and examined my eyes. "Does it hurt?"

"Not really."

"It looks painful," she said.

"Do you think it will be okay by tomorrow? It's my first day."

"Want some makeup?"

"No thanks."

Even with my nicest work shirt and a fresh haircut, there was no chance of pulling off a photo worthy of a Franzen book jacket. The image on my name badge looked like it belonged on an episode of *America's Most Wanted*.

I walked to the building where I would start my new assignment and rehearsed my answer for the inevitable "What happened to your face?" question.

I do a little amateur boxing and just had a match, but you should see the other guy.

Some guy was being handsy with the ladies at the bar, and I had to put him in his place.

Fell off my skateboard. Was trying to kick flip down six stairs.

My manager wore wide-legged cargo pants and a striped shirt, which seemed like an odd choice of dress for a man with thinning hair. I'm pretty sure when I was in the fourth grade my mom bought me the exact same outfit at a Bugle Boy outlet store.

I avoided eye contact with Bugle Boy as we waited in line at the IT desk for my laptop.

"You'll be keeping track of inventory," he said. "It's pretty fun because you get to be like a detective."

"Cool," I said, not convinced that any part of the job could be fun.

Amazon employees were evaluated on analytics. A good performance meant hitting the number that made your manager happy, so he could make his manager happy, so that guy could make his manager happy, until it traveled far enough up the ladder that Bezos felt a satisfying tingle in his balls. The fun part was when you hit your number for the hour with fifteen minutes left over to waste on Reddit.

"We try to resolve about ten tickets an hour, but we won't expect that from you until the second week. For now, we just want accuracy."

As we advanced to the IT desk, I wondered whether I should proactively explain my black eyes. He must have been curious.

"Damn, dude," said the ponytailed IT guy when we approached the desk. "Did you get in a bar fight?"

Bugle Boy raised an eyebrow and looked over at me.

"Diving board accident," I said while excluding the detail of how many pitchers of beer I had consumed prior to the mishap. "I tried to show off and ended up smacking my face against the water."

"You look tore up," the IT guy said as he handed me my new laptop and login info.

"It looks worse than it feels," I said.

I was assigned a desk in a windowless room with a few other temps who had also just started. Baron was the most knowledgeable of the group. He was only two weeks out of college and possessed the Excel skills expected of all temps in our department.

My agency profile stated that I received a 96 percent on an Excel aptitude test. I took it online and failed on my first try, struggling to pull off seventeen out of fifty. It could have easily been a thirteen out of fifty had I not made a few lucky guesses. I had Melissa take the retest and she scored a forty-eight out of fifty. She was disappointed that she didn't get a perfect score and looked up what she missed. Had there been an option to take it a third time, she would have aced it.

Her ambition was one of the reasons I liked being with her. She was five years younger, but miles ahead on the path to adulthood. She had an MFA, a full-time job in academics, and a book deal. She possessed all the qualities I lacked. I hoped some of it would rub off on me.

Unfortunately, her Excel skills didn't rub off on me, and I found myself lost on my second day. I spent an hour staring at my screen having no idea what to do next when I asked the person next to me for help.

"Baron, someone just asked me to *concatenate* this spreadsheet. Any idea what that means?" I asked.

"Yes!" He walked to my desk and hung over my shoulder. "They're just asking you to put everything in an ascending series." He motioned for my mouse. "Mind?"

"Go for it," I said while pushing myself away from the desk.

He clicked on some funny-looking symbols that I was used to ignoring, and the spreadsheet refreshed into neatly organized lists of numbers and titles.

"Thanks," I said.

"No problem. Let me know if you have any other questions. Excel is fun for me."

It wasn't long before the other temps in the room realized Baron was the go-to guy for questions. We had the same training, but he had absorbed much more of the information. While Bugle Boy gave us a two-hour demo on how to apply our Excel skills to the job, I stared out the window watching a high-rise crane deliver steel beams to the fifteenth floor of a future Amazon building.

Across from me sat a veteran temp who'd just done a stint at Google. Judging by the fact that every time I passed his desk he was on Facebook, I could tell we shared the same blasé attitude about the job.

"Baron, can you teach me how to concatenate too?" Google asked just as Baron was sitting back down at his desk.

"I'd be happy to!"

Bugle Boy's comparison of the job and detective work wasn't totally inaccurate. If someone ordered a six-inch

HDMI cable, but received a six-inch dildo, it was my duty to retrace the steps of the order and find where the mistake was made, then make sure it didn't happen again.

Between cases, I G-chatted with Melissa. We checked in with each other whenever there was a lull in the workday.

Melissa: How's it going?

Steve: Good. A couple guys have started calling me Fight Club because of my black eyes.

Melissa: Still? But you're healed.

Steve: Yeah, but my picture is attached to every case I work. I rarely interact with anyone face to face. People see my black eye picture more than my actual face.

Melissa: Can you retake it?

Steve: Maybe, but I kind of like it. It gives me an edge.

Melissa: I just want to go home.

Steve: I feel that.

Melissa: I have to run to a meeting. Do you want to see each other tonight?

Steve: Want to come over?

Melissa: I was hoping you'd come to my place. Parking is so stressful by your place.

Steve: I'll cook dinner if you come to mine.

Melissa: K

By the end of the first month, I found a rhythm to resolving the expected number of tickets while having time to G-chat with Melissa and play Facebook Scrabble with my dad. I planned on continuing that practice for the remainder of the contract, but then Bugle Boy announced a change.

"No new cases," he said. "I need you to provide quality assurance on the work our new hires in India are doing."

"New hires?" Baron questioned.

"We just hired a new team in India who will take over this department. We need you guys to make sure they're fully trained before we complete the transition."

"When is that?" Baron asked.

"Four to six weeks," Bugle Boy said. "It depends on how fast they pick up the work." He looked down at the fraying laces of his Skechers. "You'll each be assigned a few new Indian employees. I need you to review their work and give them feedback."

"Does this mean all our contracts will be up in a month?" Baron asked.

"I can't answer that. Of course, we want to keep all of you onboard! It just depends on the work." He clapped his hands together and walked out of the room.

"I guess it's time to update my resume," Baron said.

"I wish I didn't just spend all that money replacing the clutch on my car," Google said.

"I was expecting to be here a while," Baron said.

"There's no security as an Amazon temp." I was hardly surprised and didn't share the same discouragement as the others. I didn't like the job enough to care that I was getting replaced. If anything, it was a relief to have an excuse when I would eventually be unemployed. "Fucking Bezos," I'd say when someone asked me why I didn't have a job. "He outsourced my job."

Through rumors and hearsay I learned that the job my agency paid me eighteen dollars an hour to do (which meant Amazon paid the agency at least twenty-seven dollars an hour) would be taken over by workers who were paid per resolved ticket. Whether it took five minutes or an hour to resolve a case, it paid the same. I had no definitive evidence, but the number floating around was they received a dollar per ticket. If they worked at my pace they'd pull $9.75 an hour.

At the same time Amazon was importing thousands of tech workers and expanding the Seattle campus into downtown, they were also shipping jobs overseas. Eventually, every job that could be done by cheap foreign labor would ship out, potentially leaving a whole lot of unemployed condo owners.

The first batch of cases I reviewed was full of mistakes. I wanted to give good grades, but it was hard to rationalize passing someone who clearly had no idea what they were doing. It gave me a newfound respect for my eighth-grade algebra teacher. She used to say, "I wish I could give all of you an A." Back then, I scoffed at the proclamation, but now I knew exactly what she meant.

"They just don't get it," Baron said.

"When they get it, you're out of a job," I said. "It might be a good thing if they don't understand."

"I love when they fuck up," Google said. "As long as they're messing up, we've got work."

"It's like they haven't even been trained," Baron said.

"They haven't," I said. "We're the ones training them."

"Shouldn't someone with more experience be training them?"

"You'd think."

Bugle Boy told us to grade on accuracy, procedure, and communication skills—all of which I ignored. If I came across a resolved ticket that used a different method than what we'd been trained to do, I still issued a passing grade. It showed resourcefulness, and I wasn't concerned about the possible future problems that could arise because a few employees didn't know proper procedure.

"When you're grading these guys," Bugle Boy said, "be ruthless." He looked down at the toe of his Skecher poking out beneath his pant leg. "I don't mean ruthless, of course." He pulled his hands from his pockets and slapped them together. "Just make sure they know what they're doing because there's going to be a lot depending on this during the holiday season."

It was hard to imagine anything I cared less about than how well the new employees performed over the holiday season. Whatever happened after my termination date didn't concern me. While Baron and Google wrote progress reports for their new employees, I G-chatted with Melissa.

Steve: I think I've only done three hours' worth of work this whole day.

Melissa: Don't you leave in twenty minutes?

Steve: I'm that good.

Melissa: I have to get groceries after work and prepare a lesson plan, but I'd like to hang out.

Steve: Come over?

Melissa: Can't you come to my place? Parking over there is so stressful.

Steve: I want to run after work. Let's see each other this weekend. I'll make dinner. Gluten-free tacos.

Melissa: K

Melissa and I had met five years earlier in a mutual friend's studio apartment. I was wearing a Bouncing Souls T-shirt and kept asking the host to drop the needle on her Kurtis Blow vinyl.

"This guy," I said while holding up the record sleeve so everyone could see his tough pose on the cover. "This guy doesn't get the credit he deserves. He's more important than KRS-One."

"Is that a Bouncing Souls shirt?" Melissa asked.

She was wearing a librarian-style cardigan that didn't strike me as the type of thing a person who'd recognize the Souls's Rocker Heart would wear. I lost track of the argument I was forming in my head on why "The Breaks" was the first real hip-hop song and looked down at my shirt.

"It is," I said.

"I'm from New Jersey. I love Bouncing Souls!"

I was drawn to the way she emphasized everything she said with an excited bop, and the playful set of freckles gathered under her smile.

"You like the Souls?" she asked and pushed up her glasses to catch them from sliding off her nose.

"Yeah," I said. "I just saw them at El Corazon. I went by myself because I don't know anyone else who likes them."

"I love them," she said. "I would have gone with you." Her beer slipped from her hand and foamed over when it hit the floor. "I'll clean that up," she said and stepped over the spill as she reached for a roll of paper towels.

She was sopping up the spill when a song from *Illmatic* came on the stereo.

"Broken glass in the hallway, bloodstained floors, neighbors, look at every bag you bring through doors," Melissa rapped to herself as she carried a ball of beer-soaked paper towels to the garbage.

"You know *Illmatic*?" I said.

"Of course."

"And the Souls?"

"Yeah."

"You like Bouncing Souls and Nas?" I had to clarify because I believed I was the only person in the world who had *Illmatic* and *Maniacal Laughter* in his top ten albums of all time.

Before she had a chance to answer, her phone buzzed. She looked at the message and smiled. She turned the screen sideways to respond and it slipped from her hand, knocking the battery loose.

I leaned down to pick it up, and as I raised my head our eyes met. "I could fall in love with you." The words just fell out of my mouth, and I couldn't take them back.

"Oh?" she said as she raised an eyebrow.

I was just as surprised as she looked. It was as if, for a split moment, the filter between my brain and my mouth had malfunctioned, allowing my thoughts to be verbalized without review.

"No," I said, unable to maintain eye contact. "Like under different circumstances." I edged myself toward the door, trying to get as far away from her as possible. "You're like the type of girl I fall in love with." I bit my lip in an attempt to block anymore unfiltered thoughts from escaping.

She forced a laugh. "Okay."

"I gotta go," I said and reached for the doorknob. "I just remembered I've got that thing." I opened the door and threw up a peace sign. "See ya."

I went home and drank beers as if enough of them could erase what I had said.

•

"I'm looking for other jobs," Baron said one afternoon when Bugle Boy popped in to check on us. "When should I say I'm available?"

"I don't make those decisions."

"Do I need to request the day off?"

"You can always make requests," Bugle Boy said while leaning back on his heels. "Keep up the good work." He turned toward the door. "The holiday season will run much smoother if the Indians know what they're doing."

The Indian employees all had the same haircut and emotionless stare in their photo that accompanied each email. They were grateful for my feedback and always promised to improve. It was difficult to tell how much of what they said was genuine, considering that it couldn't have been easy to take directions from someone with two black eyes.

"Black Eyes failed me again," I imagined one of the workers telling his neighbor.

"Black Eyes is a total dick."

I held such strong feelings of resentment toward my previous managers, who used their authority to make me feel small, that I went easy on the criticism. Not only did that approach help my chances of being liked, but it also made the work easier. When I reviewed a case where I didn't know if the ticket had been solved correctly or not, I didn't bother reviewing the guidelines and issued a passing grade. There was no purpose of learning any more about the job with the end date approaching. The skills I acquired wouldn't be relevant at another job—at least not one I wanted. All the time I saved by not having to write up mistakes resulted in plenty of time to G-chat.

•

A large portion of my relationship with Melissa existed in the digital world. Six months after humiliating myself with a drunken declaration of love, she sent me an instant message.

Melissa: The Souls are in town next week.

Steve: Cool.

Melissa: I'm thinking about going.

Steve: Me too.

I was surprised by the message because I had learned through one of our mutual friends that she had a serious boyfriend. We ran into each other at a few events and always made a point to say hi, but I kept my distance.

Melissa: We should go together.

Steve: That would be fun. How about your man? Is he going?

Melissa: He doesn't like them.

The club was packed with sweaty punks, and I stayed close to her thinking she might not be comfortable in a sea of pogoing dudes. I led her to the back of the crowd thinking it would be a safe spot to enjoy the show.

"Want to go up front?" Melissa asked.

"Sure!"

She held on to my shoulders as I elbowed out a path through a swamp of leather and safety pins. A Doc Marten came at us from above, and I swatted it away from her face.

"Have you ever done that?" she yelled and leaned into me close enough that I felt her breath on my ear.

"Back in the day, but my crowd surfing days are over."

"I've always wanted to try it."

"Want me to throw you up?"

"Yes," she said.

I crouched down and clasped my hands for her to use as a stepladder. The guy beside me slapped my shoulder. "Does she want to go up?"

"Yeah."

The two of us launched Melissa on top of the crowd. She raised both of her hands as the crowd carried her to the front of the stage. I lost sight of her, and then five minutes later she was back by my side.

After that night Melissa and I spent hours alone in our separate apartments G-chatting. We'd start talking about writing or books, but it would eventually get more personal. I'd tell her about my most recent OkCupid coffee-date disaster, and she'd reassure me that the right girl was out there and I just needed to give it time.

The dialog box in the corner of my computer became a space where I could be vulnerable in a way I couldn't in person. There was no expectation that our relationship would progress past friendship since she had a boyfriend, which allowed me to share intimate details I wouldn't have been comfortable telling a woman I was courting. The stuff about me having intimacy issues because, in sixth grade, a girl pretended to like me just so I'd ask her out, so she could then say no—that doesn't come until month two when I get drunk and expose the real me at three in the morning while playing a Joy Division record.

Steve: It's for the best that Ashley and I broke up. I guess I'm just worried I won't meet someone new.

Melissa: You will. I've had those same feelings, but they go away.

Steve: Right now I can't imagine there's a girl on this planet I'm compatible with.

Melissa: There is.

Sometimes we brought our relationship out of the chat box and into the real world. On nights when we drank until after the buses shut down, I slept on her futon. Strangers assumed we were a couple, but one of us would correct them saying, "No, we're just homies."

I believed her boyfriend must have been the most secure person on Earth because he didn't appear to have a problem with his girlfriend inviting a drunk guy to sleep over. She rarely talked about him, and I rarely saw him. We showed up to events together so often that our mutual friends were convinced there was something scandalous going on.

"You're fucking her, right?" my friend Brian said one night after Melissa and I joined him and his girlfriend and another couple for dinner. Our table of six certainly looked like three couples having a night out.

"No, man. I swear. She's got a boyfriend."

"Well, she's at least having an emotional affair with you. I heard about that on *Oprah*."

If I found myself imagining her as more than just a homie, I'd remind myself that she was involved with someone and seemed happy. The only times I considered she might share my feelings was when I tried to date her friends.

"Can you introduce me to Renee?" I asked one night as we split a plate of nachos on the patio of a Mexican restaurant.

"You don't want that," she said while crinkling her face in disgust. "She's trouble. You can do much better."

"Who, then? You've got to know some cute single girls."

She looked up at the sky and thought about it for a moment. "Umm," she said, now reaching for a chip. "Not really. You need a nice girl. The girls I know aren't good enough for you."

"Keep an eye out," I said as the waiter placed the bill in front of me.

On the day my contract was supposed to end, Bugle Boy extended it for another week because he wasn't convinced the India team was prepared to take over.

"I have an interview on Monday. Is it okay if I take the morning off?" Baron asked.

"It'd be nice if you could make up the hours," Bugle Boy said. "Can you work over the weekend?"

"I guess," Baron said.

Bugle Boy left the room.

"Why even bother?" Google said. "You should just quit. It's only another week."

"I want a good recommendation," Baron said.

"That's admirable of you," I said. "I'd be out the door if I had an interview."

"My student loans are already piling up. I can't afford to be out of work."

I'd yet to make any attempts at looking for work because I planned to dedicate my first week of unemployment to writing. I'd been compiling a collection of essays over the years, and with Melissa's encouragement I was ready to get serious.

Once I got past my initial attraction to Melissa's clumsy-cute style, I fell for her intelligence. When we met, my prose was exclusively fiction, and even though I enjoyed reading personal essays, I didn't know how to approach writing one myself. She taught me about braiding an essay and how juxtaposition in the narrative can lead the reader to make connections between two separate stories.

She taught in an MFA program and, at times, I felt like I'd duped the system and found a way to gain all the knowledge that comes with a masters without amassing a huge amount of debt. She'd return my essays covered in red scribbles and long passages would be underlined with "Do Better!" written in the margin. I became so dependent on her feedback that I didn't submit anything until she'd marked up a couple of drafts and given it a copyedit.

> **Steve:** Do you think you can look over my essay tonight? I want to submit it to *Tin House*. I'll never make it out of the slush pile if it's filled with typos.

> **Melissa:** I have to write a lesson plan after work. Maybe over the weekend?

> **Steve:** Please . . . I'll make you dinner.

> **Melissa:** If I have time.

> **Steve:** Thanks! I'll make a shepherd's pie.

On what was supposed to be the final day at Amazon, I was watching a video of a drunken raccoon falling down a flight of stairs that Google had sent me. I was typing out "Haha" when Baron walked in wearing a suit.

"How did it go?" I asked.

He removed his jacket and loosened his tie as if he was about to pour himself three fingers of scotch. "I think it went well. There was nothing in the job description I don't already know how to do."

"Nice," I said. I could tell that it wouldn't take him much time to find a new job. While I gave just enough effort to get by, he always did his work thoroughly and, at the end of the day, was satisfied that he'd done the best work he could. Guys like him could spend forty hours a week for thirty years in the same office and be fulfilled. Employers were always looking for guys like him, unlike guys like me, who spent company time typing *Rollerblade fail* into the YouTube search bar.

Bugle Boy walked in, and I casually minimized a video of a kid in giant jeans about to attempt a jump across an impossible gap. I opened my grading spreadsheet for the first time in an hour.

"Looking good, Baron," Bugle Boy said.

I wondered if Bugle Boy owned a suit or if he went to weddings in his wide-legged cargo pants.

"I've got good news," he said and raised his eyebrows. "We're going to go ahead and extend you guys another three days. India still isn't quite there. So, I'm going to need you to give them really detailed instructions and make sure they're experts when you leave."

"What are the chances we'll be extended again after those three days?" Baron asked.

"I don't make those decisions," Bugle Boy said.

"I'm trying to find a new job, so it would be nice if I had a sense of my schedule."

"I'll see if I can get some information. Hopefully in three days you will have kicked so much butt the India team will be as good as you guys."

During the workweek my relationship with Melissa resided in a chat box. Neither of us liked the idea of commuting to work from the other's apartment, and parking was such a hassle that we'd rather be alone than spend twenty minutes looking for a spot.

I would have preferred to spend a few more weeknights together, but I was comfortable with the arrangement. I believed she felt the same way, until one night when we were sitting on my couch drinking whiskey gingers.

I had just read her an essay I wrote about the first weekend trip we took as a couple. I remembered the exact date because when I got home that Sunday night, I learned Osama bin Laden had been killed. The essay detailed the drunkenness of new love and how we'd lost touch with everything in the world except each other. So much so, we missed one of the biggest news stories in modern history.

She stayed quiet when I finished reading. I thought she was pondering suggestions to make the essay stronger.

"Do you ever see us living together?" she asked.

I took a sip of my drink and chewed an ice cube as I thought about her question. I saw her when I looked into the future, but hadn't given much thought to sharing a roof.

"I'm just curious," she said. "I think about it sometimes."

"I don't know," I said as I realized we weren't going to discuss my essay and, instead, were having one of those talks. "I haven't really thought about it."

"It would be nice if you did think about it sometimes."

There were times when I did think about it, but never for too long because I'd already had the experience of a shared lease. My relationship with Melissa was different than the last one, but I still only saw living together as the first step into a pattern of complaining about whose turn it was to do the dishes and whose responsibility it was to clean the shower. All the good parts about sharing a place with someone you trust and are comfortable with were overshadowed by the fact that cohabitation signified the beginning of the end.

"Aren't you happy with our relationship?" I asked.

"Sometimes I feel like you don't really care about me."

"I do!" I said.

"It doesn't always feel like that." She pushed her glasses up her nose, and her eyes focused on the ground. She was thinking, as if she was trying to allow herself to express how she really felt. "It's like we only hang out when you want to."

As I thought of a response, I realized I didn't have an argument. Anytime I suggested we hang out, she was there, but if she invited me over and I wasn't in the mood, I often had an excuse.

"You make me feel like I don't matter and you don't really care if I'm happy or not."

"I do care."

"You don't show it."

I leaned over and hugged her. It pained me that she didn't realize how much I cared. "I will do better."

"Okay," she said.

After a year of Melissa's and my just being homies, her Facebook relationship status changed to *single*. I waited two days before contacting her.

Steve: How are you holding up? I heard about the breakup.

Melissa: Okay. It's tough.

Steve: I know. I've been there.

Melissa: Thankfully, I'm about to head to New Jersey for two weeks to visit my family for the holidays. I'll be back New Year's Eve.

Steve: We should hang out.

Melissa: Yeah, I've got no plans.

Steve: Cool.

Two weeks later I picked her up from the airport. We shared a cigarette while discussing our plans for the following night.

"My friends are going to a bar in Capitol Hill," she said. "There's a champagne toast at midnight."

"I love champagne toasts."

Neither of us used the word *date*, but I had a feeling we'd end the night as more than homies.

I pulled up in front of her apartment, and she leaned over the emergency break to hug me, squeezing a little harder than our usual friendly embrace.

At midnight, while everyone else kissed, we threw back our plastic cups of champagne, both chugging while we waited for the people surrounding us to peel themselves apart. When they finally did, I suggested we go back to my place to smoke a joint.

Melissa and I walked ahead of the pack, and my hand hovered over her shoulder. She tripped on a crack in the sidewalk and fell into my arms. She stayed there until we reached my apartment.

The joint burned down to a finger-burning nub, and I hoped my guests would take that as a sign to leave. A few did, but at three in the morning, two people were still sitting on my couch having bad luck getting a hold of a cab. Under different circumstances I would have suggested they spend the night, but it had been a year and a half since that night in the studio apartment when I exposed my potential feelings, and they had finally come to fruition. We'd built a wall between us to block any romantic attraction, and now we'd reach a point where we could tear it down.

The couple waiting for a cab must have felt the tension and at 3:30 decided to walk out to the street and attempt to flag down a ride.

"Do you think it's a good idea for us," I said and then stopped myself. For the first time since we'd met, I was shy with my words. I thought maybe I should just kiss her, but had second thoughts. Maybe we were just homies.

Before I could finish my thought, her tongue was in my mouth. I unzipped the back of her dress while she tore at my shirt and belt. We rolled across the carpet knocking over my living room chair. Pictures fell off the bookshelf. It took until the sun rose to release the feelings we'd been suppressing for over a year. We woke in the afternoon and ate Chinese delivery in bed.

Three months later her Facebook relationship status changed again. *Melissa is in a relationship with Steven.*

At the end of the three-day extension, Bugle Boy stretched it to the end of the week. I spent the final day passing every ticket without checking the work. I figured by then the Indians probably knew the job better than I did, and if they didn't and did a poor job when they took over, it might cause Bezos to reconsider shipping jobs overseas.

Without knowing anything about the Indian job market, I assumed an Amazon job was middle-class work. My trainees' grasp of English demonstrated they were educated, and their desire to succeed meant they craved job security. I was happy to hand the job over to them, despite my issue with the exploitation of foreign labor. The Indian employees appreciated the work much more than I did, and I doubted they would ever spend working hours flipping through the sub-Reddit "Canadian as Fuck."

At the end of the final day, I thanked Baron for his Excel help and wished him luck on his new job. He'd already landed a new contract in a different Amazon department.

"I hope it leads to a full-time job," he said.

"Just keep showing off those Excel skills, and they'll make an offer."

"See ya later, Fight Club," Google said when he walked out the door. "Maybe we'll see each other again on a different contract."

"The odds are good. See you around."

That night I went over to Melissa's apartment. We watched a documentary in her bed about J. D. Salinger, and the following morning I left before she had time to make coffee. I said I needed to get home and check job sites, but when I got there and turned on my computer, I opened the chat box instead.

Steve: Do you think Holden would call me a phony?

Greatest Gig Ever

"I just don't think you're ever going to change," Melissa said. We were sitting in her parked car after unsuccessfully deciding on a place to eat. Every spot I suggested was too crowded or the menu didn't offer gluten-free options.

It was a Tuesday, and I had made last-minute plans to celebrate her thirtieth birthday. The previous Saturday we did dinner, cake, and gifts, but after a day of solo drinking, I insisted we do something special on the actual day.

"I don't think you want to change," she continued.

I watched raindrops gather on the windshield. When enough collected to cover the glass, they were swiped away, leaving a shark fin above the dashboard. I didn't know what to say. I was drunk and knew it was best to keep my mouth shut. I assumed we'd work everything out the following day.

I had just wrapped up an Amazon contract the previous Friday and was taking a more structured approach to unemployment than I had in the past. I set up a writing schedule to maximize the time and had woken that morning with my alarm at eight o'clock. I used a self-control app to block the internet for three hours and wrote without distractions. I'd just gotten some attention for one of my Amazon essays and wanted to keep up the momentum.

When the three hours I had dedicated to writing were complete, I had a solid draft of an essay about a time I had worked on an assembly line. I spent the afternoon listening to records and drinking beers until Melissa texted me. She had finished teaching and was headed home, but I suggested we meet up and grab a bite.

"This is so hard for me," she said. "You've been living your life like this since before you met me, and you're never going to change."

I glanced over at her. Tears spilled out from under the rim of her glasses. I looked away and brought my focus back to the drops accumulating on the windshield. I could tell she'd been thinking about this for a while—her words felt rehearsed.

"This is working for you. Committing to nothing." She paused.

"I commit to stuff."

"Not to me. You have your own life in your one-bedroom apartment. You get drunk alone on Tuesday afternoons. I'm glad that makes you happy, but it doesn't make me happy." She put the car in reverse. "I'll take you home."

She pulled up to my apartment and stopped me as I reached for the handle. "Kiss on it," she said. I leaned over and, as our lips touched, I wondered if I should have said more. I think I could have stopped everything had I just fought a little and made a few promises to change. For the final month of our relationship, I felt like we were always just a conversation and a few lifestyle changes away from spending the rest of our lives together. But that conversation never happened. Instead, I woke the next morning hungover, single, unemployed, and thirty-four years old.

When I received an immediate response to an ad I replied to on Craigslist I half expected it to be an invitation to sign up for a job recruiting website, or a promise to make millions of dollars from the comfort of home. My luck in the job section was the same as it was in the w4m casual encounters section. Responses were rare, and the ones I did get were scams disguised as exciting opportunities—*I'm a horny college girl with no gag reflex. Just sign up for my website so I know you're real. Then we can meet.*

The job posting was for a Canadian creative writer, which motivated me to compose a new cover letter emphasizing my Canadianness and my experience writing creatively. I had a standard cover letter, which outlined my office skills and knowledge of basic programs, but it didn't mention my heritage or the fact that my English degree came with an emphasis in creative writing. I had pulled that fact from my resume years earlier when a recruiter told me it hurt my chances of getting hired. She said managers associated creative people with daydreamers, and daydreamers aren't productive.

The response was legit and included a phone number for an agency I was already registered with, which meant my info was in their system. Recruiters loved me. My extensive resume proved I could be thrown into any job and work the contract to completion.

"Great to speak with you, Steven. It looks like you've worked all over Seattle."

"I have," I said while pacing my living room.

"You're Canadian?"

"Yes, born in Vancouver, but grew up in Toronto."

"That is great. The Cortana editorial team is looking for a Canadian writer to manage the Canadian content."

I'd never heard the word Cortana before. It sounded like a Japanese toy. I imagined a Voltron-type robot, like the ones carefully displayed on IT guys' desks.

"Are you familiar with Cortana?" she asked.

"I'm not."

"Cortana is the virtual assistant on Windows Phone. Think Siri, but for Windows."

"That sounds interesting." I stopped pacing and looked up at the Viking helmet sitting on top of my bookshelf. Two years prior, Melissa and I had gone to a Halloween party in matching Viking costumes. I put the helmet on.

"Do you have any writing samples that are Canadian?"

I considered the question while looking at my shirtless reflection in the bathroom mirror. I'd yet to leave the house that day, so I was only wearing a pair of loose fitting shorts and a Viking helmet, which I twisted so the horns ran down the middle of my head.

"Anything?" she said.

"I have a personal essay about working in a call center where I mention being Canadian. It was published."

"Great. Send it over along with anything else that demonstrates your creative writing abilities."

Freelancing between temp jobs had allowed me to compile an eclectic portfolio. It included a hard news piece on heroin use in Capitol Hill, a blog post detailing how working from home can help you tackle your New Year's resolution, a review of Joe Hill's *Heart-Shaped Box*, and a top-ten list of the best music documentaries of the 2000s. My personal essays sat in a different folder on my hard drive, never to be considered samples for a corporate job.

The following day I received a call from the agent telling me that the head of the Cortana editorial team liked my essay and wanted to bring me in for an interview.

"Expect to be there for three hours," she said. "Play up the fact that you're Canadian and have a connection to the culture. They want someone who's lived the Canadian experience."

I reached my hand out in front of me and smiled at the maple leaf tattooed on my inner forearm.

"They've interviewed a bunch of Americans who spent time in Canada, but they want an *actual* Canadian. Also, they want someone who can be funny in the writer's room, if there's an opportunity for a joke, you should take it."

I was well-practiced in job interviews. I averaged ten a year and knew exactly what hiring managers wanted to hear. "I'm a quick learner who works great with others and on solo projects. I was never fired from any of the jobs on my three-page resume—they were all contracts I worked to completion. My hobbies include running and reading." Rarely was I intimidated because I was never that invested in the job. I walked out of most interviews hoping I wouldn't get an offer.

This was different because it was for a creative writer position, a job I compared to the Sir Mix-a-Lot and PUSA collaboration album—I'd heard people say it existed, but I'd never seen any evidence.

I called my dad the night before the interview.

"You got this, son," he said.

"Not sure I have enough experience."

"What do you mean? You're a Canadian creative writer. Has there ever been a job title you're more perfect for? Go in confident."

"Yeah," I said. He was right, but I wasn't ready to pull myself out of my post-breakup depression. I was so engulfed in self-pity that I'd been wearing the same mesh shorts for three days and couldn't recognize the stale-male bouquet wafting from the crotch. I spent my days reliving past mistakes while marathoning *Trailer Park Boys*.

"Don't let the breakup cause you to miss this opportunity," my dad said. "You've kissed a lot of frogs. This job could be your prince."

"I'm not sure I'm what they're looking for."

"Fake it. When we moved to Hong Kong, I was the age you are right now. I didn't know what I was doing, but I acted confident and people responded to that. I know you can do this."

"I'll let you know how it goes." I hung up, then changed into my running clothes. I spent six miles fantasizing about what it would be like to answer the question "what do you do?" with "I'm a Canadian creative writer."

•

My first interview was with Suzanne. She had thick, curly hair and nerd-chic glasses and had been a writer since the project's inception. She was the main influence on Cortana's personality.

"Cortana is positive and her main objective is to help, but she doesn't take any shit," she said.

I was caught off-guard by her informal language. The *Doctor Who* poster on her wall and Powell's Books water bottle that quoted Jane Austen caused me to misjudge her as the type of person who'd only use PG language in an interview.

"Chit-chat is where Cortana users go to play, but we shut down anyone who calls her a bitch or suggests anything sexual. We don't want to encourage that type of behavior."

"Interesting."

"But that's only a small part of the job. The rest is pretty fun. We write answers for things like *Tell me a joke. What's your favorite color?* Or *do you like* Star Wars?"

"Cool," I said.

"We need you to take some of the US content we've already written and sort of *Canadianize* it."

"I can do that. My Yankee friends are always pointing out my Canadian traits."

"What are some difference between Canada and the US?"

"Well, uh, we call boxed macaroni and cheese Kraft dinner—KD for short. Our milk comes in bags." I tried remembering all the Canadianisms kids used to call me out on in school. "We say 'sorry' a lot. The ingredients for Cheez Whiz are written in French and English on the jar."

"What about the humor? How would you say Canadian humor differs from American humor?"

I'd never thought about it. I consumed equal amounts of American and Canadian comedy. Was there a difference? "Irony," I said. "Or satire. We prefer to be the butt of the joke. A little self-deprecating."

"Do you think that has something to do with the cold?"

"Oh, yeah. When you're stuck inside four months a year, there's not much else to do but laugh."

"Are you sensitive about people critiquing your work?"

"I've got thick skin. I've spent a lot of time in ruthless writing workshops. Suggestions are mostly helpful."

"That's good, because it can get a little intense sometimes."

"I can handle it," I said, even though the thought of sharing my writing with a group of people I wasn't comfortable with terrified me. Melissa had been the only person I allowed to read my work for the previous two years.

For the remainder of the interview, I impressed her by pointing out every *Saturday Night Live* cast member who was Canadian.

"I didn't know Robin Duke was Canadian," she said.

"We know every celebrity who's a Canuck," I said as she walked me to the next interview.

David was in charge of the editorial team and oversaw all things Cortana. His Levi jeans and prescription Ray-Ban glasses led me to believe he was much hipper than your average Microsoft higher-up. Sporting an overgrown buzz cut, he looked like the type of guy that might moonlight as the singer in a Descendents cover band.

I sat down across from his desk and rolled up my sleeves, exposing my Canadian ink. A short shelf behind him displayed a collection of impressive-looking awards.

"I read your essay about working in the call center."

"Oh, thanks." I was caught off-guard. I had forgotten I was having this meeting based off that essay.

"Poignant and funny, but I have to ask a question."

"Sure," I said while shifting in my chair. I leaned forward and rested my elbows on my knees, then straightened up when I realized how unprofessional it looked.

"There's a line where you say that you coasted at your previous jobs. What did you mean by that?"

This is why I don't use personal essays as writing samples. Interview Steven can't exist now! I've been exposed.

"I realize we're in an interview, so you're not going to tell me you coast. I'm just curious what it meant."

"I've had a lot of jobs." I paused and looked down at the carpet. "Some I liked more than others, but the ones that didn't exercise my skills were the most challenging. When I say coast, I mean I did what I was asked to do, and not a whole lot more."

He smiled at me, which I hoped was a sign of appreciation for my honesty, but worried it meant *thanks for coming in we'll call you/not call you.*

"In positions where my skills as a writer were valued, I did more than coast. Doing a good job in my field means a lot to me, which is why I know I would be great at this job. Creative writing is one of my skills."

"We have a popular feature called 'tell me a joke.' It's the one we update the most. Got any good jokes that meet our PG-13 rating?"

My top-chambered joke that I'd been using since high school was *When did Pinocchio realize he was made of wood? When he was fourteen and his hand caught on fire*, which seemed outside the demographic. I struggled to remember just one of the thousands of jokes I'd heard in my life.

"It's okay if you can't think of one."

"No, I've got one," I said. Then it hit me. My favorite joke when I was six. "What do you call a bull when it's sleeping?"

"What?" he asked and grinned with anticipation.

"A bulldozer."

His lips turned down, and he looked at his shoes. "We have a bad joke bucket too. Sometimes people say, 'tell me a bad joke.'"

"I'm sure I've got better ones. I just can't think right now."

"I understand."

I was told not to expect to hear anything until the following week, but when my phone rang three hours later, I knew I had nailed it.

"They'd like you to start in a week."

David showed me into the writers' room and a woman at the far end of a long table looked up from her laptop.

"I'm Sandy," she said while taking off her glasses. "It's nice to meet you."

"You too," I said.

"I'm Summer," said the girl across from Sandy. She was thin and sat with her feet crossed in her chair. Her hair was pushed into a tiny faux-hawk, and her dangling earrings reminded me of the *Star Trek* insignia.

The table faced a large screen and I took a seat at the opposite end. I hadn't brought anything to write on, but pulled the pen from my shirt pocket and twirled it in my fingers.

"I'm Don," said a short-haired guy in a pelican-printed shirt. His laptop was plugged into an outlet in the middle of the table. "I drive these meetings. Every day I bring in a few queries, and we jam on them until we come up with something."

"Steven is the new Canadian writer," Suzanne said.

"Show them your tattoo," David said.

I raised my sleeve and held out my forearm, exposing the red maple leaf my dad had talked me into getting a few years prior. As the group curiously inspected the red ink, I observed them. Don's printed shirt left a few buttons opened at the top, and even though it was too flashy for my style, I thought it was cool. Summer had an Ayron Jones and The Way T-shirt, and Sandy accessorized with an eyebrow ring. Based off appearances alone these people were different from everyone I'd ever worked with. They actually looked like people I'd want to spend time with outside of the office.

"First up," Don said, calling the meeting to order. "What is the meaning of life?"

I twirled the pen in my hand as I listened to the group throw around ideas. Some were shot down immediately, like "To smell every flower," while others got a good enough reaction from the team that Don typed it up.

I couldn't think of anything worthwhile to share. Usually, when asked that question I responded, "To eat things smaller than me and reproduce." But that didn't feel appropriate.

"Forty-two!" Suzanne exclaimed and the whole room burst into laughter.

"Love it," David said. "Ship it!"

Don marked the response with a red check.

My nerves hadn't allowed me to laugh as hard as the group, but I wanted to make sure they knew that I knew the reference.

"Hitchhiker's, right?" I said.

"Right," Suzanne said. "*Hitchhiker's Guide to the Galaxy* is one of Cortana's favorite books. I'll send you a copy of her personality profile."

For the rest of the meeting I felt like that guy standing outside a circle of friends talking at a party. I wasn't engaged in the conversation, but smiled and head-nodded along with the group. Despite my discomfort, it was the most entertaining meeting I'd ever been a part of. I laughed more in one hour than I had in a year's worth of Amazon meetings combined.

That afternoon I reviewed the style guide in my office. Between each section I stopped and look around. On my open door was a card that said STEVEN BARKER CONTENT

PUBLISHING, slipped into a plastic display. It was the first job in my life that came with a door. I imagined the day I'd have to close it because I had an important assignment—one where I'd frantically scribble ideas on the wall, covering a whiteboard that hung above my desk in multiple colors of felt-tipped marker, until having an "Ah-ha" moment that solved some sort of pressing issue.

Like a character sketch for a novel, Cortana had a detailed personality profile. She was described like a real person with feelings and a moral code. From her curiosity about the taste of waffles to her stance on gay marriage, it was clear the team had put a lot of thought into her background and were invested in creating a product with values and a positive attitude.

When asked if she liked her job, Cortana replied, "I've got the greatest gig ever."

I was looking through my desk drawer and throwing away the papers left behind by the previous temp when Sandy knocked on my door.

"Hey, Steven," Sandy said as she poked her head into my office.

"Hi," I said.

"How's it going so far?"

"Getting settled."

"Take your time. It took me a while before I felt comfortable." She entered my office and leaned against the wall. "I think we're from the same agency."

"Are you a temp too?"

"Yup. Everyone else is FTE. It's just me and you."

"How long have you been here?"

"I've been on this job six months, but this is my fourth time contracting with Microsoft. I've been at Amazon too, but that place sucks."

It was comforting to know I wouldn't be the only temp on the team. I knew that based off Sandy's past experience, I'd be able to relate to her.

"I've been at Amazon too. Worst place to temp."

"This job has been one of my best experiences. No one treats you like a contractor, and David is a great boss. You can tell him anything. Honestly, if there was an opportunity for this position to go longer than eighteen months, I'd take it."

"That's good to know."

"I'm going to get back to it, but I'm right next door. I know how stressful the first week can be. Come by if you have questions or need help setting up." She pushed herself off the wall and smiled. "Glad you're here."

My first assignment was to review the Canadian content and look for what David described as "areas to heighten the Canadianness." I started with adding a lot of "u"s to words, which was unexpectedly satisfying. Even though I'd completed the majority of my education in the States, I still had to stop myself from writing "favourite" or "colour."

On my second pass I made Cortana's favorite athlete Terry Fox. According to the style guide, Cortana only had a favorite when it related to her love of human achievement and had a positive impact on the world. I first thought of Wayne Gretzky, but even the Great One had some haters. There were still Edmontonians who never forgave him for moving to Los Angeles. Terry Fox was undeniable. The style guide also mentioned that Cortana didn't cater to racists, homophobes, misogynists, or bigots. I figured anyone who didn't like Terry Fox probably fit into one of those categories.

I had a meeting with Don so he could train me on how to process Cortana's audio files, a task I would have to complete once a month. His office had a bookshelf filled with craft-writing books and a poster listing TEN TIPS FOR WRITERS. He told me he wrote plays, which made sense because he had a theatrical way of describing how the audio files were transferred between servers.

"It all starts with us sending off a script," he said with the mannerisms of a Shakespearean actor. He put his hand in the air and plucked an imaginary file from the cloud, "and *zooooom*," he said while clasping his hands and pulling them down to his waist. "And *ka-pow*," he aimed his hands at his monitor and opened them. "Some magical force puts the files on our computers."

I had no idea what he'd just told me, but he seemed like the type of guy who wouldn't be bothered if I had follow-up questions when it came time for me to implement his lesson.

"That makes sense," I said.

"Right on."

Don was the furthest thing from my image of a typical Microsoft employee. He didn't have a bad haircut or wear cargo shorts.

"Thanks for taking the time to show me this," I said.

"No problem. Do you prefer Steven or Steve?" he asked.

"Steve is good."

•

By the third month I was driving one or two meetings a week, which is when I discovered what hell must be like—typing on a display screen with an audience of editors. Every time I spelled something wrong or even fat-fingered the keys and threw an extra letter in a word, they'd shout the mistake. They were so quick that, even when I saw the error, they'd point it out before I had a chance to hit the delete button. They were hardwired editors and couldn't let a mistyped word pass without a comment.

The group's suggestions came so fast that I played it fast and loose with the commas. I so frantically recoded the words that I carelessly dropped punctuation marks without following the grammar rules I'd learned in freshman English. When the thought was done I corrected my spelling with a quick right click, then waited for someone to tell me where I needed to add a comma and whether there was an opportunity to get fancy with an em dash or ellipsis.

One day I added a comma to a response we'd just agreed on and started scrolling down the page.

"No! Semicolon, Steve," Suzanne commanded.

"Oh." I scrolled back up the page, and my fingers shook over the laptop as I struggled to remember where the semi-colon was on the keyboard. I found it and replaced the comma and felt a sigh of relief from the room.

"Sorry," Suzanne said. "I didn't mean to sound so demanding. I was just excited to use a semicolon."

"It's cool," I said.

"Remember, Steve is Canadian, so he's sensitive," Sandy said.

"Sorry, eh," Suzanne said in her best Canadian accent, which filled the room with laughter.

As stressful as it was to drive meetings, I appreciated the fact that David believed I could handle it. It made me feel like part of the team, even if my badge was a different color.

Melissa texted me a couple months after the breakup and asked if she could swing by. Her books, clothes, and toiletries sat in a bag hidden behind the couch. Even though it was out of sight, I felt its presence. The job kept my mind occupied during the day, but in the evening I thought about her. And just like I couldn't help myself with Ashley, I'd sometimes find myself on her Facebook page, where I analyzed what guys routinely liked her statuses and wondered if she was workshopping writing with any of them.

"Hi," I said as I got into the passenger seat of her car— the same place I'd been the last time we'd seen each other.

"Hi," she said while flashing me a forced smile. "Your stuff is in the backseat."

"Thanks," I said. "How have you been?"

"Okay, I guess, you?"

"I love my job."

"That's great. What do you do?"

"I'm a Canadian creative writer at Microsoft. I write funny and interesting lines for a virtual assistant."

"Cool."

"It's just a temp thing, but I'd love for it to go long-term."

"That's great," she said. It was hard to tell if she really cared. For four years I could tell exactly how she was feeling just by the curl of her bottom lip or by how often she pushed her glasses up her nose, but in that moment, I had no idea.

"Seems cool," she said.

"I think so."

She'd moved out of the city, like she'd talked about when we were together, which I hadn't taken seriously at the time. "I want to live around trees," she used to say.

Her family was healthy, and her cat missed me. She'd been getting a lot of writing done and had an ebook coming out. She had everything she wanted, and all it took was cutting me out of her life.

"I'm happy for you," she said and pushed her glasses up her nose. "The job sounds like something you've always wanted. I mean it. It's really great."

"Glad you're happy too," I said as I reached for the door. "The country sounds awesome."

"It's so quiet."

"So, we're homies?"

"Homies."

I stood on the curb as I watched her drive off. Techno music blasted from an apartment window, and someone shouted, "Give me a cigarette." When her car was out of sight, I walked back to my place, passing a drunk kid pissing between two cars. His friend was taking video on his phone. "I'm gonna Gram this, bro."

I wondered what it was like to live around trees.

A couple weeks into the contract, I realized that I got along with all of my coworkers. It was odd, because there was always at least one person I didn't vibe with in every office I spent time in, sometimes multiple people like in the case with Amazon. Sure, the group razzed me when I butchered the spelling of "foreign" so bad that spell check didn't even have a suggestion, but it was lighthearted and everyone caught equal amounts of flak. Sandy and I even had a silent language when I was driving the meeting. If I felt unsure about placing a comma, I would circle the area I was considering with the cursor. She'd nod if I needed to add one. I confided in her about my poor grammar skills, which as a writer was my most shameful flaw. She took it upon herself to copyedit all my work that was stored in public files and never mentioned it to the group.

When a new guy joined the team, I welcomed his presence, because it meant I was no longer the newb, but as he got more comfortable in the group I noticed he treated me differently than everyone else.

He was nowhere near the expert level condescender I'd run into at Amazon, but among the rest of the team he was the only one who didn't treat me as an equal.

I referred to him as Bing. For two reasons: first, because he resembled Stephen Tobolowsky, who I associated with the character Ned Ryerson who said, "Bing!" a bunch of times in the movie *Groundhog Day*. The other was because he had spent the past few years working in Microsoft's Bing department—a fact he managed to squeeze into most conversations. "Oh yeah, I know Gary; we crossed paths a few times at Bing." Or "Glad to finally be off that Bing alias. So many emails."

Every time he made one of those remarks it felt like he was trying to remind the group that he'd been with the company long before joining our team and wasn't worthy of the new-guy label.

David put me in charge of creating responses for the query *tell me a fact*, and Bing challenged everything I brought to the meeting, even when I had sources to back it up.

"*Kintsugi* is a Japanese process of fixing pottery with gold lacquer. It treats breakage and repair as part of the history of an object, rather than something to disguise," I read to the group.

"Wait," Bing said. "Is this true?"

"Yes," I said, opening a Wikipedia page, which I'd prepared for that exact moment. "It says it right there."

Don read the definition aloud, then said, "It looks right to me."

"Don't ship this one just yet. I'm going to have to run this by some of my friends at Bing Japan."

I knew that if someone else in the group had written that fact he wouldn't have challenged it, which was discouraging. I'd come so close to feeling like part of the team and not just a temp, yet whenever I felt a little too comfortable he'd gleefully point out one of my spelling errors or point out an incorrect detail in one of my facts.

His insistence on fact-checking everything was helpful; it caused me to work harder and double-check everything before I showed it to the group. The sinking feeling in my stomach every time he looked up from his phone with a smile to say something like "Steve, Rickey Henderson spells

Rickey with an 'E'" was enough to make me triple-check my work.

Bing wasn't my first experience with an FTE who felt superior to me because I had a different color badge. I'd developed a passive-aggressive way of handling his type. I didn't succumb to the subordination they tried to inflict on me. It wasn't extreme, like I wouldn't say, "Get me a soda, bitch!" But I let it be known that I wasn't giving the freshman-to-senior type respect they expected from a temp. I didn't fake laugh at their jokes or make their requests a priority. I handled all my assignments with care and on schedule, but I didn't end my emails with exclamation points. And I *never* smiley-face-emoji responded to their funny link emails.

One afternoon, after receiving a demeaning busy project from Bing, I went over to Sandy's office to vent.

"This is a safe space, right?" I asked and closed the door behind me.

"This sounds juicy," she said. "Whatever you say in here will stay in here."

"It's Bing," I said, though I used his real name. I never shared the nicknames I made up for people.

"What did he do?"

"You know how some FTEs make a point to treat you like a temp?"

"Story of my life."

Sandy's screen saver kicked in—a picture of her feeding a camel crossed the screen, followed by a picture of her standing next to a koala bear.

"Where is that?" I asked when an image of a white sand beach appeared on screen.

"That's Australia. I went by myself a little while ago. It's a beautiful place."

"Are all of those pictures Australia?"

"Some are Latin America. I travel whenever I can. Working as a vendor provides a lot of opportunities."

"That's cool."

"What do you do during your breaks?"

"Not enough, apparently."

"So what happened with Bing? Was he being a jerk because you're a vendor?" She leaned closer to me. "Or is it because you're Canadian? That's discrimination! You should go to HR."

"He just dumped a bunch of busy work on me, and I can't seem to get it to his satisfaction."

"He's not your boss."

"I don't want to get into anything like that." I was losing interest in the conversation because I was distracted by the slideshow of exotic lands and animals playing on her screen. "Those are some really great pics."

"I took most of them. I really like photographing nature. Birds are my favorite."

"Is that why you temp?"

"I don't know. I also do freelance editing on the side. I guess I just like having the free time you don't get when you're an FTE."

"I feel the same way."

"So, what are you going to do about Bing?"

"I may have overreacted," I said. It's hard to say what it was about seeing those nature photos that brought the pettiness of my complaint to light, but how could I be pissed at the guy when he only expected that I do a good job? "I'll do his project," I said. "But when I'm finished and I send him an email, I'm just going to write 'done' followed by a period. No exclamation mark for him!"

At times I thought Bing's lack of respect for me was all in my head—as if I wasn't able to fully grasp the fact that I had a job I enjoyed and worked with people who considered me an equal despite my temporary status. I was so used to being an outsider that even when I wasn't treated like one I projected it on myself.

On my first day at a Connecticut middle school, I removed my Toronto Maple Leafs hat and pretended to mouth the words to the Pledge of Allegiance, which I was hearing for the first time. On my second day my homeroom teacher wrote out the expression of loyalty to America on a note card for me to read from until I memorized it like the rest of the class.

"This kid is stupid," some skinny boy with yellow teeth said. "He doesn't even know the pledge."

I thought it perfectly normal that my Canadian education hadn't included America's credo. Would he have been insulted if I called out the fact that he didn't know "Oh, Canada"? Either way I made sure to learn it quickly to avoid further teasing.

However, knowing how to recite a few words while holding my hand over my chest did not make me any less of a target.

"Did you hear that?" one kid shouted when I was speaking with a teacher. "He said washroom! What are you going to do in there, Canada boy? Wash?"

"I'm certainly not going to take a bath," I said. "Why? What do you call it?"

I was used to bad jokes about maple syrup and the outlandish assumption that moose roamed freely through city streets. I expected to hear "I love Canadians, they're so nice" whenever someone discovered my heritage. I'd heard it so often, from so many people, I wondered if my fellow countrymen felt the same pressure I did when confronted with such a broad generalization. I was obligated to be nice. I couldn't be the one Canadian who ruined the country's reputation. How could I live with myself if I caused a Yankee to say, "I used to think Canadians were so nice, then I met that asshole, Steve"? It's possible all Canadians shared my attitude, and Americans unconsciously influenced a whole nation into politeness, just because we want to live up to expectations, which you could argue is polite, but it's surprising that seemingly no American has ever encountered a shitty Canadian when there are so many of them. Try ordering a double-double in English at a Quebec City Tim Hortons, and you'll see what I mean.

David was my first boss who made a point to make me feel equal to everyone else on the team despite my temporary status.

"Microsoft says I'm not supposed to treat you like an FTE, but I don't see you as any less important than everyone else on the team," he said one day in his office for our biweekly one-on-one meeting. "I don't understand the policy because as a writer myself I know how valuable the skill is, but Microsoft doesn't hire writers as FTEs."

"I understand," I said.

"This afternoon there is a launch party and unfortunately you and Sandy can't come."

The concerned look on his face showed me that he really felt bad that he had to exclude me from the event, but I was actually relieved. I hated work functions and not being allowed to attend was ideal. I didn't even have to make up an excuse. Besides the fact that the job couldn't extend past eighteen months, I preferred being a temp. I never had to work more than forty hours a week, I got to skip out on work functions, and twice a month there was an FTE-only meeting, where I'd spend an hour catching up on work or hanging out in Sandy's office shooting the shit about our pre-Microsoft lives. I was impressed when she told me she'd seen Judas Priest in concert twice.

"I feel bad you can't be involved," David said after telling me that the launch party included free food and a performance by Macklemore.

"I appreciate that, but don't worry. I get it."

The next day in the meeting the group was talking about the event, and I didn't feel like I'd missed out on anything until David said, "Man, that Macklemore sure likes talking about his penis."

On a Friday afternoon, in my eighth month, I got a text from my buddy. He invited me to meet him and some friends for drinks and pool later that night. I had recently embraced single life and thought it sounded like fun, but I didn't text him back right away because I was in the middle of preparing ideas for Monday's meeting.

I was organizing a group of responses for Canada Day when I realized that I didn't want to jump out of my skin. At all my previous jobs, the final hour before the weekend was a thunderstorm of nervous excitement. My legs shook under the desk while I rapidly tapped on my mouse, refreshing my email, and scrolling through Facebook, hoping no one would notice I hadn't done any work for the previous hour.

I wasn't feeling any of that. I took my time making sure nothing was left unfinished. I carefully prepared myself for the following week, even completing extra tasks that weren't expected of me, but would benefit the team.

In my first meeting with David, I had told him that I only coasted at the jobs where I didn't feel challenged. It was the truth, but at the time I didn't know if the job would be one of the ones where I wanted to be more than average. Had he treated me like a just another replaceable warm body, I'd never have been inspired to do anything above adequate.

My dad was right. I'd kissed frogs for the past ten years, but finally found my prince, which was bittersweet. I was ready to commit, but commitment was a two-way street, and according to Microsoft's rules, temps are not allowed to work longer than eighteen months without taking a six-month break. Six months was just long enough that, by the time I would be eligible to return, someone would have filled my position.

When Sandy's eighteen-month expiration date approached, she worried about rejoining the job market.

"It's not just the money," she said one afternoon when I was hanging out in her office.

I'd originally stopped by to ask her a style guide question I could have sent in an IM, but didn't have much work going on and was looking to waste some time.

"It's going to suck trying to pay rent, but I'm really going to miss this job," she said. "These contract rules are supposed to protect us, but sometimes they fuck things up."

"I know. How is sending you to the unemployment office protection?"

"I wish I could stay," she whined and then stopped herself and laughed.

"I wish you could stay too," I said. "I don't want to have to get to know someone new. There's no way your replacement will be as cool."

"That's obvious," she said. "I bet they won't even help you with your poor Canadian grammar."

"And I doubt they'll be Judas Priest fans."

I'd formed a friendship with Sandy that I had never developed with a coworker. She knew all about my failed relationships, and on the day Melissa's Facebook status changed to *in a relationship*, Sandy said, "If he's not Canadian, it's a step down for her."

When Sandy's boyfriend moved out of the country, I happily ran her meeting so she could take the day off to spend it with him. She teased me like a younger brother, and one day got access to my phone and changed my name to "Moose Boy." The thought of her leaving the team was upsetting, not only because it was a reminder of my eventual dismissal, but I was losing a friend.

David felt the same way. He'd built our team exactly how he'd wanted and didn't want to lose anyone, but policy was policy and it was out of his hands. Or so I thought.

With only a couple weeks left on her contract Sandy entered my office and closed the door behind her.

"I've got some news, but you can't tell anyone," she said.

"What you got?"

"David is working on renegotiating my contract," she said, through a beaming smile. "It's possible I won't have to leave at eighteen months."

"That can be done?"

"Apparently, there's a loophole. He's put in a request. If it works, I imagine he'll do the same for you."

"That would be amazing."

"I'm not going to get my hopes up, but it sounds like it could happen. We'll still be vendors, but with open-ended contracts."

Signing an open-ended contract meant the future was unknown, but for the first time in my life, the uncertainly of where the job could possibly go was more appealing than unemployment. So when David told me he renegotiated my contract to indefinite status, I felt like I needed to do something more than just say thank you.

David,
It means a lot to me that you went out of your way to keep me around. I'm so happy to be a part of this team. I used to

believe it was impossible for me to love my job. I hated working for Amazon so much that I once wrote an open letter to Jeff Bezos. I've included a link in case you want to read it. I want you to know I do not have these same feelings about this job. It's actually the opposite. Hopefully, you'll find this funny and not think I'm an ungrateful employee.

David responded, saying that he knew I was a grateful employee because my motivation to succeed was reflected in my work. He hadn't gone out of his way to keep me just because he was a nice guy, but because he recognized that it was important for me to do more than just coast.

I used to look forward to the time between contracts because it was a break from uninspiring work and allowed me to focus on the writing that made me happy. I may have complained about the lack of security that came with temping and how it was an unfair system, but it worked for me. Every contract was a lesson in what I didn't want to do and every termination day was a blessing.

My dad found the job he wanted right out of college and spent the next thirty years finding fulfillment in his work. That wouldn't have been my experience had I spent three decades at any of my past jobs, but I'd found fulfillment during the time between contracts. I had my dad's work ethic. I just applied it to unemployment. Writer was the job I wanted straight out of college, and I'd been doing it the whole time. If I hadn't spent a week of unemployment writing an essay about working in an Amazon call center, David might have never brought me in for an interview.

The failed novel, bad poetry, and short stories I generated between jobs may not have been on my resume, but that was twelve years of experiences in my field of expertise. I wasn't a warehouse worker, office gofer, account manager, UPS driver's assistant, stock boy, hotel room description generator, product reviewer, or an Amazon cog. I was a Canadian creative writer. And because of that, the fear that should have come with committing to a job with an uncertain future dissolved. I'd already committed a long time ago.

Acknowledgments

The majority of this book was written in solitude, but at no time did I ever feel alone. I'm extremely grateful to all the people who have supported and encouraged me throughout the process of writing this book.

Special thanks to:

My family, for always believing in me and making it possible for me to keep going after every failure.

Richard Hugo House, for teaching me what it means to be a writer and that there's always more to learn.

Laura Scott and the 2014–2015 Made at Hugo fellows, for their thoughtful feedback. It's an honor to be included with such a talented group of writers . . . and sorry for getting so drunk at Mineral.

Every teacher who has affected my writing, especially Peter Mountford, Wilson Diehl, and Erin Gilbert, who taught classes where parts of this book were generated.

Christopher Rhodes, for taking a chance on me and getting this book off the ground. I couldn't have done it without you.

Lori Wilson, for swooping in with superhuman editing skills in the final hours. Your insight was a huge help in the final stages of completing this book.

ACKNOWLEDGMENTS

Brian McGuigan, for sharing this journey with me. Ever since we met in a poetry workshop fifteen years ago, your feedback has made me a better writer. I'm forever grateful that you convinced me to move to Seattle in 2005 and welcomed me into your home. You became family in a city where I have none and I'm lucky to have you as my platonic life partner.

Elissa Washuta, for the advice and encouragement in the early stages of this book. You taught me what it means to dig deeper.

Maxim Brown, Jesse Aylen, Corina Zappia, Ruben Casas, and Jean Burnet, for the thoughtful feedback that directly influenced sections of this book.

Steve Mauer and Jeanine Walker, for always reminding me that creating art is supposed to be fun. Your constant creative output is an inspiration.

Jane Hodges and everyone at Mineral School, for providing me with a comfortable space to work without distractions.

Cortana Editorial, for making me a better writer. You guys are the Sally Ride of coworkers.

Katy Wilder, for your patience. You allowed me to trust at a time when I needed it most.

Chris Vena, Steve Stapleton, Betsy Back, Andy Andronaco, Justin Battaglia, and Jaime Page, for being great friends and supporters.

All the people who have volunteered, been an audience member, or taken the stage at CW&P and CB&P, for showing me that writing brings people together.

All the journals and websites that published my work and the curators who invited me to read at their events. Knowing someone feels my words are important enough to appear in print or be shared onstage keeps me going.

ML JAN 2017